"*With Open Ears* is sheer delight. The [...] ries, biblical truth, and application [...] deeper, sweeter understanding of God [...] ever changed the way I perceive sound—from something taken for granted to something spiritual in nature, a gift that gives me a glimpse of my heavenly Father's heart."

—GRACE FOX, Bible teacher and award-winning author of *Finding Hope in Crisis*

"Karen Wingate writes from a unique and personal perspective to guide readers to a deeper awareness of God's presence in our everyday lives. *With Open Ears* offers devotions that are thought-provoking and inspiring, steeped in Scripture, and sprinkled with humor. The author clearly shows us the meaning of Psalm 46:10: 'Be still and know that I am God.' I look forward to the next thunderstorm."

—CRYSTAL BOWMAN, award-winning author of more than one hundred books, including *I Love You to the Stars*

"*Distracted*. That might be the word that best describes our current culture and personal experience. Our senses are overwhelmed by so many sounds that the voice of God gets muffled. Jesus frequently said, 'Whoever has ears, let them hear.' We have ears, but what do we hear? Who do we hear? Too often we hear the lies of the Evil One. And one of his greatest temptations is to simply overwhelm us with noise to distract us from hearing God. Karen Wingate's book *With Open Ears* is a powerful reminder that we need to be attentive to all the ways God communicates and speaks to us. She encourages us to slow down and truly listen to the voice that fills our souls and gives us life. Use this book as a daily devotion and then prepare yourself to use your ears to really hear."

—GLEN ELLIOTT, pastor, coach, and consultant in Tucson, Arizona

"In her book *With Fresh Eyes*, Karen taught us what it's like to see through the eyes of a woman born blind. In *With Open Ears*, she teaches us to use our God-given sense of hearing to experience the world—and God—in ways we might never have experienced before. As I read Karen's thoughtful work, I sensed him saying, 'Are you listening?' Thanks to Karen, I am."

—LORI HATCHER, author of *A Word for Your Day*

"Karen Wingate has done it again. *With Fresh Eyes* opened our eyes to the love and mercy of God seen in everyday life. Now, in *With Open Ears*, Karen ushers us into God's presence, encouraging us to listen to his voice in the natural world, in the people and circumstances that surround us, and within our own hearts. This compelling book puts us in touch with the marvelous world we live in and the marvelous Creator who made it for us."

—SHAWN MCMULLEN, editor of *Christian Standard* and author of *Coming Home to Holiness*

"Most of us are surrounded by sound every day, but when was the last time we saw it as a gift? Do we realize God is speaking to us through the things we hear, like the rain, the bird's song, and our own breath? In her book *With Open Ears*, Karen Wingate focuses on five different aspects of sound and how they testify to God's divine presence in our lives. This book provides refreshment to weary travelers who need to be reminded of the simple yet beautiful gifts surrounding us each day. If you're looking for a book to reinvigorate your faith and help you sense God's presence in fresh new ways, look no further."

—ABBY MCDONALD, writing coach, contributor to Proverbs 31 Ministries' *Encouragement for Today*, and author of *Shift*

With Open Ears

60 Reflections on the Wonder of Sound from a Woman Born Blind

KAREN WINGATE

KREGEL
PUBLICATIONS

Cataloging-in-Publication Data is available from the Library of Congress.

ISBN 978-0-8254-4884-3, print
ISBN 978-0-8254-6391-4, epub
ISBN 978-0-8254-6390-7, Kindle

Printed in the United States of America
25 26 27 28 29 30 31 32 33 34 / 5 4 3 2 1

*In memory of
Grandpa.
Your loss of hearing taught me
to value the gift of sound.
Your faith and courage taught me
to never give up.*

Contents

Introduction. 13

Part One: Sound Design—What We Hear
1. Breath 19
2. Rain. 23
3. Thunder. 27
4. Waterfalls 31
5. Falling Trees 35
6. Birdsongs 39
7. Woodpeckers 43
8. Barking Dogs 47
9. Voices. 51
10. Babies 55
11. Laughter 59
12. Crickets 63
13. Night Owls. 67

Part Two: Sound Hearing—How We Hear
14. Household Hums. 73
15. Horse Hooves. 76
16. Open Spaces. 80
17. Tour Guides. 84
18. Sermons 88
19. Longing to Belong 92

20. Fuzzy Sounds 96
21. Ear Rings 100

Part Three: Sound Information—Why We Hear

22. Doorbells. 107
23. Directions 111
24. Airplanes 115
25. Sirens 119
26. Footsteps 123
27. Teakettles 127
28. Tornado Warnings 131
29. Implosions. 135

Part Four: Sound Communication—Who Hears Us

30. Ancient Words 141
31. Radio Transmissions. 145
32. Words of Grace. 149
33. Words of Comfort 153
34. Words of Truth 157
35. Idle Chatter 161
36. Information Overload. 165
37. Unwholesome Talk 169
38. Complaints 173
39. Loving Discipline 177
40. Rumors 181
41. Blame Games 185
42. Testimonies. 189
43. Instruction 193
44. Gentle Words 197
45. Breaking News 201
46. Witty and Wise Words. 205
47. Love Notes. 209

Part Five: Sound Celebration—What God Hears

48. Musical Expression 215

49. Songs of Praise.................................... 218
50. Rhythm and Repetition 222
51. Laments... 225
52. World Languages................................. 229
53. Praise Prompts................................... 233
54. Notes of Encouragement......................... 237
55. Wind Chimes..................................... 241
56. Music Groups 245
57. Off-Key Notes 249
58. Heart Melodies.................................. 253
59. New Songs 256
60. Trumpets.. 260

     My Prayer for You 265
     Acknowledgments 267
     About the Author 271

Introduction

*God's voice thunders in marvelous ways; he does
great things beyond our understanding.*
JOB 37:5

Sight and sound.

We need both to interpret our world. Both equip us to understand the God who created all that is within the world and who longs
to communicate with us, his highest creation.

Yet our senses are so intricately woven into our physical makeup
that we forget the wonder behind what we see and hear. We don't notice when our car runs smoothly, but the slightest rattle or thump gets
our attention. In the same way, we don't pay attention to the steady op-
eration of our senses—like eyesight or hearing—until they don't work.
They're so much a part of our physical design that we often accept our
senses as the way things ought to be. We forget to marvel in wonder at
what we can see and hear, and we fail to remember that our senses—in
fact, our very lives—are a gift, not a right.

I know I have.

If you read my first book, *With Fresh Eyes*, you danced in joy with
me over my experience of Better Than Ever eyesight. We looked at
stars, clouds, sunsets, and geese. We deliberated over what our eyes
saw, analyzed what the seen told us about God, and praised him for all

11

he has done. Together we appreciated the finer details of this visually oriented world.

As friends old and new observed my excitement about experiencing improved eyesight and then saw the world through the wonder I expressed, they often reacted with, "We take so much for granted." Their renewed wonder bounced back toward me as I, in turn, learned to praise God more. We fed off each other's joy and excitement.

What a beautiful world. What a great God.

In the wonder, that phrase—"We take so much for granted"— reverberated in my brain. Had I done the same with God's other gifts?

Had I not discredited the value of the gift of sound?

I defended myself. As a visually impaired person, wouldn't I of all people know the benefits of hearing? Hadn't I used my hearing to compensate for my lack of vision all my life?

Some have the mistaken idea that God gifts those who cannot see with high-powered hearing. Not true. That would be like saying God gives hearing-impaired people 20/10 vision, and my deaf friends will tell you that's not true. When you lose one sense, you realize the usefulness of other senses. You have to. Necessity is the mother of invention and discovery.

What a beautiful world. What a great God.

Learning to use my ears to hear what others could see became such a part of my life that I didn't stop to think about it. So accustomed to hearing because I *had* to hear, I did not pause to appreciate the gift. I took hearing and sound for granted.

After I wrote *With Fresh Eyes*, I determined to use the same approach that had helped me discover the expanded horizons of my eyesight to now find the wonder within sound. I laced intentional listening into my day. I paused and paused some more. I leaned in to listen for what

I could hear, to separate the layers of sounds that were too often camouflaged by my own noise. What else could I hear? How did the sound change? What made it change? Why was it important for me to hear the undertones and countermelodies of sound?

And the core question I asked so many times as I discovered new aural horizons was this: What does this tell me about God my creator?

The discoveries shocked me. Sound, I observed, might be more intricate than eyesight. The interworking of vibration, physiology of the ear, and auditory processing of the brain are so precise, instantaneous, and multifaceted, only a creator God could make them so. The setup is too complicated for simple evolution to perfect through billions of years of trial and error.

The best combination of sounds, I decided, is spoken language. Sound is the basis of communication, and God wants to relate with us in ways we can understand. So he arranged sound into spoken word and gave us the gifts of language, speech, communication, and music. Yet, like any of God's good gifts, we either use sound to honor him or abuse it to serve our own purposes and hurt others created in God's image. We are responsible for the sounds we insert into our corner of the world—how they honor God, encourage others, and build God's kingdom here on earth.

If my life is centered around exalting the God of creation, then I will want to use the gifts of both sound and hearing to honor him. That's what I hope this book will do, for you and for me—that, together, we will experience the wonder of sounds that exist and become better at using those sounds to celebrate the God who loves us.

In the following chapters, you and I will discover that God inserted sound into his design for the universe so creation could sing his praise, tell of his mighty power, and provide information that enables us—his highest creation—to live safe, productive, and wholesome lives. He hard-wired us with the ability to hear and make sounds of our own so he could communicate and interact with us, and so we could distribute the gift of his love to those around us. The glory and value of sound, as described in part 5, comes full circle in God's gift of music—a gift we access to praise him and encourage each other. It's the instrument he will ultimately use to call those who've chosen to trust and honor him to their eternal home.

So come stand beside me. Let's open the door to God's world and turn our ears to the opening. What do we hear? Through hearing the sounds God has made, we'll discover more of who he is, how he works, and how we can glorify him. May God open our ears to the sounds around us so that through them, we can hear his voice and know him better than ever before.

PART ONE

SOUND DESIGN
What We Hear

1

Breath

By the word of the LORD the heavens were made,
their starry host by the breath of his mouth. . . .
He spoke, and it came to be; he commanded,
and it stood firm.

PSALM 33:6, 9

*T*he dream faded, and my sleepy brain found comfort in normal
night sounds. But something wasn't right. I couldn't hear my husband's snoring.

Isn't that a good thing?

No, my bleary brain told me, I should have heard the subtle whiff
of his CPAP machine. Had Jack snuck out of bed because he couldn't
sleep, hoping not to wake me?

Being the good soulmate that I am, I didn't want to wake him either, so my fingers crawled toward his bedspace. My compassion and
curiosity turned to concern as I made T-shirt contact. He was still
in bed. I tensed. I knew of spouses who had found their loved ones
dead in the middle of the night. Was he all right? Pressing against his
shoulder, I felt the rise and fall of his chest and heard the sound I was
listening for. A deep breath whiffled through his CPAP mask.

He was alive. The sound of his breathing told me so.

Breath is the essence and symbol of life. We cannot live without it. Breath bookends life. A baby's first breath wails into a cry, announcing that new life has come. Breathing becomes ragged and uneven in the death rattle of life's final hours.

The sound of breath is the sound of life. And life means there is a person, a sentient being, cradling that breath of life. Without breath, we could not speak, move, or function, for breath provides the elements the body needs to live.

It has always been this way. It was so from the beginning. In fact, God's first gift of creation was given in the form of a breath. "Now the earth was formless and empty, darkness was over the surface of the deep, and the Spirit of God was hovering over the waters," says Genesis 1:2.

My preacher husband tells me that the Hebrew word for *spirit* can also be translated as "breath." It makes sense, for breath is audible. The sound of a breath indicates the presence of someone even if we can't see them. At the beginning, breath over empty space announced the presence of God.

Six days later, God breathed life into the first human. "Then the LORD God formed a man from the dust of the ground and breathed into his nostrils the breath of life, and the man became a living being" (Gen. 2:7). Think of it! The first sound Adam heard was the breath of God. The breath coursing through his lungs had come from the mouth of God—his very essence.

It's true for us too. Each breath we take comes directly from God. It is a mark of his image, for no other life-form contains the breath of God. The sound of a human breath is more than the sound of life; it is the sound of God's presence within human life.

The breath of God makes us different from the rest of creation. Even the way we express ourselves through our breathing shows that God has created us to be interactive and emotional beings. Think of how we can communicate our emotions with the sound of a breath. A contented sigh after a good meal. A gasp of surprise. An inhale of uncertainty as we debate whether we should say what's on our mind.

Rapid breathing that reveals fear or anxiety. All of these breaths bear witness that we are different from the rest of creation, even more like God than we are like the world we live in.

Each breath we take comes directly from God. It is a mark of his image, for no other life-form contains the breath of God.

And then, Jesus breathed the breath of the Holy Spirit on his disciples, strengthening their connection to God all the more (John 20:22). The breath of the Holy Spirit signified a new kind of life, the beginning of imperishable life. God's presence—the breath of the eternal—was now inside each disciple. It was a down payment on Jesus's promise that he would always be with them. Yes, and so much more. He was with them and within them.

Breathe in. Breathe out.

Do you feel it?

God is there. Inside you.

I don't think I can ever listen to my breath again without being overwhelmed that God is inside me. I listen to my husband's soft breathing in the quiet of night and realize that a bit of the holy lies beside me. It's not mere earthly human life; it's God's life, God's desire to be a part of me and have me be a part of him. With every breath I hear from myself and the human next to me, I can hear life, and I remember the giver of life who longs to have eternal intimacy with each of us.

If God feels far away, take a deep breath and then release it, remembering that he is as close as your next breath. He knows everything happening to you. If he is sustaining your breath, your life, he has plans and purposes for you, and he's not leaving you.

If you can hear yourself breathe, you can hear God.

Tell God you are glad he is that close to you. Because he is.

Lord, thank you for life, for all that life breath represents,
and for the gift of hearing that allows me to listen to it.
Thank you for this symbol of your presence that shows you
are always with me.

LISTENING WITH OPEN EARS

Take several deep breaths. As you exhale, say aloud, "God is here."
Imagine his presence all around you.

2

Rain

*Ask the LORD for rain in the springtime; it is the
LORD who sends the thunderstorms. He gives
showers of rain to all people, and plants of the
field to everyone.*
ZECHARIAH 10:1

Jack and I sat close together on our side porch, watching rain-laden clouds mushroom in the southeast. Large drops pelted our corrugated aluminum roof, sounding like random shots from a pellet rifle. "Here it comes!" I said, excitement in my voice. It would be the first significant rain of that year's monsoon season in Arizona.

The rain stopped suddenly, like someone turning off a water line valve. *Well*, I thought, *maybe no rain for us today.* The storm would probably twist sideways and go elsewhere, and our locale would get what we call a "six-inch rain"—raindrops six inches apart. But then the rain morphed into sheets of tiny droplets that sounded like buckets of water sliding across the roof. Wind-driven rain slammed into trees, danced down the street like a parade of marching marionettes, and cascaded into a thousand miniature waterfalls. The wind took on a frenzied sound, and we bolted for safety inside our home.

You often hear rain before you see it. The initial patter on the roof and splatter on the windows compel you to peek outside and announce, "It's raining!" And the assorted emotional reactions pelt your mind as fast as the first raindrops.

"Good. We need rain."

"Again?"

"There go my plans for the day."

"I hope we get enough to settle the dust."

Before you react to your next rainfall, stop. Listen to the sound. Let your imagination run free. What does rain sound like to you?

The sizzle of bacon in a hot pan?

A crackling campfire?

A murmuring mist that lulls you to sleep or makes you want to grab a book and cuddle under a cozy blanket with a cup of cocoa?

God sends the rain in whatever form it comes. He sends it to refresh the earth, cause living things to grow, and bring fruitful harvest. If you challenge farmer friends who have endured seasons of drought about why they like rain, they'll look at you like you're an alien from another planet. Rain is an essential part of earth's life. Plants—a farmer's livelihood—wither and die without it. No rain means no plants and no profit.

> God sends the rain to refresh the earth, cause living things to grow, and bring fruitful harvest.

How interesting, though, that God creates different kinds of rainstorms. We'd all like the gentle, constant shower that evenly waters our gardens and regulates itself to fit our day planners. But God, in his unbounded creativity, makes both gentle rain and raging thunderstorms. He varies the amounts from the tease of "raindrops six inches apart" to a true six-inch gully washer that overflows into streets and basements.

Through the sound of rain, God reminds us of himself. In his final instructions to the Israelite people, Moses, the Old Testament lawgiver, made this comparison: "Let my teaching fall like rain and my words descend like dew, like showers on new grass, like abundant rain on tender plants" (Deut. 32:2). Elsewhere, the prophet Isaiah compared the influence of God's Word to the impact of rain: "As the rain and the snow come down from heaven, and do not return to it without watering the earth and making it bud and flourish, so that it yields seed for the sower and bread for the eater, so is my word that goes out from my mouth: It will not return to me empty, but will accomplish what I desire and achieve the purpose for which I sent it" (Isa. 55:10–11).

Like rain, God's Word refreshes our souls, provides the environment we need to grow and flourish, and produces the harvest fruits of holiness and righteousness that bless both us and those around us. We need regular interaction with God's Word.

But like the ebb and flow of rainstorms, the flow of God's Word into our lives isn't constant or consistent. Regular, daily Bible reading is best, but we all know it doesn't always happen that way, and that's okay. Sometimes, we feel like we're learning so much, we can't contain it. Other times, we enjoy that steady stream of daily devotions and savor weekly sermons and Bible study groups. And in still other seasons, we feel like we've entered a dry period; we must rely on what we've already learned, and we become stronger in the remembering.

I remember a drought period in my life. Stuck away in a small town for a college internship, I had little contact with other Christians. I couldn't find a nourishing body of believers. I became thirsty. I longed for the refreshment of God's Word. For the first time, I read an entire book of the Bible—the gospel of Mark—in one sitting. Grasping the big picture of Jesus's ministry replenished my thirsty soul and helped me grow in new ways. My season of drought motivated me to crave and pursue the renewal that could come only from his Word.

The sound of rain is not such a bad thing, for rain can remind us of God's infinite ingenuity in providing for survival on this earth. It also reminds us of the purpose of his Word: to teach us who he is and how we can grow to be more like him.

Lord, thank you for replenishing our world with rain and refreshing our lives with your holy Word. Thank you that, as rain waters the earth and brings new growth, your Word will accomplish your purposes.

·········· LISTENING WITH OPEN EARS ··········

The next time it rains, pause what you are doing and listen. How would you describe this particular rain? How does it parallel a weather pattern in your life? What tools do you see God using to help you grow?

3

Thunder

The LORD sits enthroned over the flood;
the LORD is enthroned as King forever. The LORD
gives strength to his people; the LORD blesses
his people with peace.
PSALM 29:10–11

*D*uring our years of family life in North Carolina and later in northeast Ohio, our Labrador retriever predicted incoming storms better than any weather forecaster. Before I could detect the first murmur of thunder, my ninety-pound dog would crawl into my lap, trembling and moaning.

Riley was no wuss, I had to remind myself. He was living up to exactly what God had created him to be. There's a verse in the Bible that tells me he was fulfilling his God-given capacity for announcing approaching storms (Job 36:33).

Me? Being the free agent God created me to be, at the first rumble my human ear could detect, I'd dump the dog off my lap and bolt outside to enjoy the show. I'd make up metaphors for what the rumbles sounded like: *The clouds are grumbling. A train ambles to the south.* Certain sharp cracks would make me picture the wind and rain splitting the sky open in advance of their nosedive to the earth below. When my imagination faltered, I grabbed what I'd heard others say. My grandma once told me the potato wagons were coming. Grandpa said the angels were bowling.

And every show was different. Some electrical storms featured cloud-to-cloud lightning accompanied by a persistent low rumble. Other times, my husband and I would count the number of seconds between the flash of lightning and clap of thunder, reluctantly reentering the house when the time lapse was under five seconds apart.

(Or not. Free agents can be known to take foolish chances.)

Why risk my own safety to stand outside and listen to the sounds of a storm? Because to me, thunder proclaims power. Thunder in and of itself can't hurt anyone, but it's the voice that announces the motion and energy happening within a storm-filled sky. Thunder testifies of the power of God. In fact, Bible verses like Psalm 29:3 suggest that thunder is the voice of God: "The voice of the LORD is over the waters; the God of glory thunders, the LORD thunders over the mighty waters."

Thunder testifies of the power of God.

If thunder is the voice of God, I wonder if the rumbles we hear show tremendous restraint on God's part. Were we to hear his full and unabated voice, we would—and should—be terrified. When Moses prepared for meeting God on Mount Sinai to receive the Ten Commandments, God descended on the mountain, accompanied by thunder, lightning, smoke, fire, and an earthquake. It was not entertaining. The record says, "When the people saw the thunder and lightning and heard the trumpet and saw the mountain in smoke, they trembled with fear. They stayed at a distance and said to Moses, 'Speak to us yourself and we will listen. But do not have God speak to us or we will die'" (Exod. 20:18–19).

Thunder and lightning remind me of the power of God. They remind me that nature contains forces I cannot control, energies so potent that if their power was fully unleashed, they would zap me into nonexistence.

You and I need this mind prompt of thunder. We need to remember that God is God, and we are not. He controls everything; we do not. And when we feel helpless to change what's wrong in the world or to fix difficult circumstances in our lives, the rumble of God's voice in the oncoming storm assures us that he is still in control. He will bring justice to the earth, and he has the authority to alter what seem like unchangeable situations.

My dog, with his inbred instincts, had it right. He trembled at the voice of God—and so should we. As humans made in God's image, we can do even more. We can put language to our trembling and articulate who we revere. We can stand in the temple of his creation, watching and hearing the oncoming storm, and cry "Glory!" (Ps. 29:9). We can proclaim the greatness of God, for the rumble of thunder speaks with his powerful voice.

Unlike the Israelites, we don't need to retreat in terror at the thundering voice of God. For God's love is as mighty as his power; his love is wide and deep, far-reaching and strong. When we experience the power of his unfailing love for us, the sound of thunder can suggest a new metaphor, each rumble repeating the chant, "I am here! I am here!" The commanding announcement of his powerful presence reminds us that God is still in charge, he is available to share his strength with his people, and he has come to bless us with peace.

Lord, thank you for creating thunder to remind me of your voice of sovereignty. You are powerful, more powerful than any part of nature. I'm so glad you are; for your powerful love and goodness will sustain me through all of life's storms and chaos.

·········· LISTENING WITH OPEN EARS ··········

Read all of Psalm 29 and Job 36:27–37:7. What does the sound of thunder tell you about God?

4

Waterfalls

Why, my soul, are you downcast? Why so disturbed within me? Put your hope in God, for I will yet praise him, my Savior and my God.
PSALM 42:5

On our way home from a restful vacation in upstate New York, Jack and I debated whether we should stop to see Niagara Falls. We were both tired and anxious to get home, and it was a dreary, gray day, not conducive to seeing the falls in all their glory.

I had seen the falls once before and made another attempt at persuasion. "We may never come this way again. It's worth the sight, even on a cloudy day."

We turned off the interstate and headed toward Buffalo. As we reached the entrance to the park, the clouds lifted and the sun sparkled on rain-kissed grass. As soon as we opened the car door, the distant roar of the falls greeted us, the volume intensifying as we walked closer toward the Niagara River's edge. We could no longer hear each other without shouting.

Jack wanted to take the Maid of the Mist boat ride, while I opted to stay on the bridge overlooking the falls and watch him get wet. To this day, he remembers the surround-sound effect as the boat paused in the center of the pool, encircled on three sides by the Canadian Horseshoe Falls. His awe-filled description makes me wish I had gone with him. "It was all-encompassing, overpowering," he told me.

We can both still hear the echo of Niagara Falls within our memories of that day. The sheer volume of water, cascading over the rocks and falling over 180 feet below, creates a constant, thunderous sound that masks all others. You can't tune it out or ignore it; it demands your full attention, awe, and amazement.

Our visit to Niagara reminded me of another moment we spent at the base of a waterfall, this time in Bear Canyon, north of Tucson, Arizona. Weary after weeks of hard ministry, we left the children with my mom and trekked over one of my favorite childhood hiking trails to Seven Falls. This series of falls is not as impressive or overpowering as Niagara, but the rumble is the same, quieter but equally intense. We could hear the sounds of other hikers splashing in the bottom pool, but the roar of the falls usurped our attention. For over half an hour, we sat in the sunshine, letting the sound sift the strife of the past few weeks into the sand at our feet. And we felt cleansed.

I wonder if the Sons of Korah, attributed as the writers of Psalm 42, experienced the same feeling of stress leaving their bodies as we did when we sat before Seven Falls. It's quite possible the Banias Falls in upper Israel inspired the writing of this achingly beautiful psalm; in fact, the psalm takes on a new dimension if you read verses 6–7 with the image of a waterfall cascading in front of you:

> My soul is downcast within me;
>> therefore I will remember you
> from the land of the Jordan,
>> the heights of Hermon—from Mount Mizar.
> Deep calls to deep
>> in the roar of your waterfalls;
> all your waves and breakers
>> have swept over me.

Waterfalls have a way of putting life in perspective. Unlike storm-clad thunder, this presentation of God's power comes in the form of a steady roar. The surround sound of relentless force reminds us that God is constant. He will always be in control, and like the never-ending pulse of Niagara and Seven Falls, God's power is lasting and present.

God wants—demands—our constant attention. Not because he is selfish and arrogant; far from it. Our creator God, who perceives everything about us, knows that his prevailing presence in our lives will strip the stress and calm the sorrow of our world-weary souls. He longs for his voice to cancel out all other voices so that, despite the chatter and whine of the world's ways, we will find peace through our focus on him. He invites us to sit in the sunshine of his care or dare to row out into the middle of his surround-sound love and experience how great and awesome he truly is.

> The surround sound of relentless force reminds us that God is constant. He will always be in control.

The constant roar of his presence calls us to put our trust and hope in his enduring, all-encompassing voice. By day, he directs his love toward us, and at night, that song stays with us (Ps. 42:8). Whenever the shifting sands and slippery rocks of life taunt us toward distress and depression, we can replay the steady, thunderous sound of the waterfall and find our hope in the One whose voice prevails.

He alone is our God and our Savior. And he's not going anywhere.

If you teeter on the edge of despair, if you feel like trials are washing over you, churning the sand at your feet and threatening to pull you under, pause and listen to the sounds of a waterfall. God is still with you. He controls everything, and he is worthy of your hope and dependence on him.

Let his voice be the one you hear above all others.

Lord God, you are more powerful than the mighty rush of waters within a waterfall. Thank you for being capable of handling anything I face and overwhelmingly in control of all that happens in this world.

LISTENING WITH OPEN EARS

Read Psalm 42. Think of a waterfall you have seen and heard. How does it remind you of the power and presence of God?

5

Falling Trees

You have searched me, Lord, and you know me.
You know when I sit and when I rise; you perceive
my thoughts from afar. You discern my
going out and my lying down; you are
familiar with all my ways.

PSALM 139:1–3

Home from another out-of-state trip, I grabbed a suitcase from the car and headed into the covered breezeway that connected our garage with the main house. Something seemed wrong. Although the sky held a thin cloud cover at high noon, the corridor felt unusually dim, especially on the north side. I looked out the window toward our back yard and gasped.

One third of our beautiful shade tree had split off from the main trunk and fallen toward the house, nestling in the inner corner that connected the breezeway with the garage. A bent gutter was the extent of any damage. But how had this happened? Neighbors told us there had been a bad storm several days before; evidently the wind in the storm had split the aging tree.

Then we wondered—had no one noticed our fallen tree? We weren't there to hear it. And our property sat between two church campuses, so it was doubtful anyone else heard it either. My quirky mind grappled with the classic philosophical question: If a tree falls in a forest and no one is around, does the tree make a sound? If no one was around to hear my falling tree, had it even been audible?

My brainy husband says it's a matter of physics versus perception. Yes, a falling tree causes vibrations, but it takes ears to perceive the sound the vibrations create.

But I'm the argumentative type, so I wonder: Would the same apply to the *sight* of a falling tree? If no one *sees* the tree fall, does that mean the image of a tree falling doesn't exist?

Sounds silly, doesn't it? You might be wondering, *Can't you two find anything better to discuss?*

Let's return to the sound of falling trees.

What about the birds, bugs, and badgers? Wouldn't they sense the vibration from a falling tree? If a deaf person stood in the forest, wouldn't that person be aware of the shaking ground from the crash of timber?

What about God?

Here's my point: If God is aware of the tiniest sparrow falling to the ground (Matt. 10:29), does he not also hear the crash of a tree? And if he hears the thud of a broken bird or a severed tree limb, how could he miss the cries of his beloved children whom he loves and cherishes beyond measure (v. 31)?

I have moments when I feel like no one hears my heart's cry. I suspect you have them too. We wonder: If no one pays attention, is our concern important? Worse yet, are we not worth being listened to?

Often, one of the greatest fears of the elderly is that they will fall and no one will know. They'll lie on the floor, hoping someone will notice the silence. They may hesitate to cry out, not wishing to waste energy on a shout no one will hear. They may feel that their cry, like the tree, has no sound, and something with no sound might as well not exist.

But we have this assurance: *Nothing escapes God's notice.*

He hears our cries. He sees our brokenness. He is instantly aware when even the weakest and least-known among us bend, break, or fall. He knows what has happened, what is happening, and what will happen. You are important and he hears you. He will respond. And he will stay with you.

If God hears the thud of a broken bird or a severed tree limb, how could he miss the cries of his beloved children whom he loves and cherishes beyond measure?

The book of Genesis records the beautiful story of Hagar, Sarah's maidservant, that tells how God heard Hagar's weeping as far away as heaven. When Sarah and Abraham sent Hagar and her son into the desert wasteland, God's angel called to her from heaven. "What is the matter, Hagar? Do not be afraid; God has heard the boy crying as he lies there" (Gen. 21:17). Abraham and Sarah were to be the patriarch and matriarch of God's chosen people; yet God also responded to Hagar's anguish. If God cared so much for a servant woman who was not part of his chosen people, he will reach down and care for any of us. He will hear.

As the Bible repeatedly emphasizes, God is attentive to our cries. For example, God's Word tells us, "The righteous cry out, and the Lord hears them; he delivers them from all their troubles" (Ps. 34:17). And Psalm 55:17 says, "Evening, morning and noon I cry out in distress, and he hears my voice."

The next time you or I hear the split of a tree limb midstorm or the sound of branches beating against our home in the darkness, we can pause to thank God that he hears, that he cares about what is happening, and that he will respond by providing whatever we need. No falling tree, no human voice, is inaudible to him.

Nothing escapes his notice.

Lord God, thank you that you hear every sound creation made it and you maintain it. Thank you for the reassurance that you also hear my cry when I am distressed and feel small. Nothing is too small for you to see.

·············· LISTENING WITH OPEN EARS ··············

Read the story of Hagar and Ishmael in Genesis 21:8–20. Why was Hagar sent away? What did God say to Hagar? How did he take care of Hagar and Ishmael?

6

Birdsongs

*All your works praise you, Lord; your faithful
people extol you.*
PSALM 145:10

 y photographer husband drives me crazy. We see a pretty sight
 and his first response is to whip out his cell phone and take
twenty pictures, cajoling me to photobomb at least five of the photos.

"Can you just enjoy the moment?" I once asked in exasperation as
we stood before an ever-evolving sunset.

He aimed his phone at me. "I am."

I complicate the moments as much as he does. When I look at the
sunset, my mind goes into overdrive with questions about what I'm
seeing, questions I'm certain only Google and Wikipedia can answer.
Inevitably, as I delve into the information I want to know about the
scenes and sounds before me, the moment passes and the sunset fades.

Birdsongs especially bring out this curiosity in me. I often hear the
song before I spot the singer. And, oh, how our fine-feathered friends
are good at making their presence known! If extroverts are defined by
how much they talk, songbirds could be considered the extroverts of
the animal kingdom. Especially the rowdy bunch at the first touch of
dawn that personify the term "early bird."

When I hear birdsongs, frustration compounds with curiosity to steal the moment. *Where is that bird?* I wonder. *I can't see it. What kind is it? Is that a mating call or a bird spat? Or is he just singing his little heart out because he wants to?* Before my Better Than Ever eyesight surgery, I could not see birds midair, in a tree, or on the ground. I could only hear their songs, and that frustrated me. Now, although my improved eyesight allows me to see birds at the bird feeder, I see their form and a flutter but not much more. This distresses me even further, for I still cannot identify the source of the sound.

Surely, if I took the time to do a Google search or consult an aviary docent, I could learn all the birdcalls and identify the species by sound. Don't completely blind people recognize birds by their calls? One blind friend tells me no, she can't. She can only identify the obvious ones, like the coo of a dove or the honk of a goose. *But I still want to know!*

My heart squeezes with compassion for my friends who are losing their hearing and say the ability to hear birdsong is one of the first to go. This should make me appreciate the early bird chatter or late afternoon lullabies more. But it doesn't. I hear a sweet warble and I strain forward, my brain, eyes, and ears striving to take it all in. I grab my phone to record the moment so I can zoom in on the photo and figure it out later.

Can you just enjoy the moment?

In my effort to focus on what I cannot see and figure out what I do not know, I forget to listen to the sound of the song. To be still and know that God is God, designer of the bird and composer of the melody he put in their throats.

> In my effort to focus on what I cannot see and figure out what I do not know, I forget to listen to the sound of the song.

None of us have cornered the market on knowing, seeing, or hearing. One day, as 1 Corinthians 13:12 assures us, we will fully understand everything just as God has known everything about us. But for today, we can take what we do know, incomplete as it is, and use it to discover God. If I cannot hear, I can marvel over what I am able to see. And if I cannot see, I can revel in the song.

Whatever I can see, hear, or know about what sits in front of me, the pivotal question is this: What does this tell me about God?

1. He is infinitely and extravagantly creative.

I had viewed the lavish love of God in the color variety of the sunset through my newfound vision. Now my ears listened for the intricacies of sound I heard on my daily walks, a mere sampling from over nine thousand bird species, each with their own unique set of calls. Scientists say a chickadee has at least sixteen varied calls, depending on the situation.[1] A mockingbird can learn up to two hundred cadences from other birds or nature sounds in order to confuse predators or lure a mate with a prettier song.[2] God didn't hold back in his countless designs. He combined sight and sound to create infinite combinations.

2. He is a God of beauty, precision, and practicality.

As I now pause and listen to the songbirds, I'm amazed at the variation of pitch, tone, and timbre. The perfected rhythm. The effortless vocalization. No voice training. No advanced degrees in music. The birds sing because God created them to sing. And each song has a function. I've learned that bird-watchers can guess what is happening in a bird's life by merely listening to the song. A series of loud chirps indicate a predator is nearby. A lovely song in spring probably means a male is wooing his lady friend; a more insistent song tells the competition to stay away.

---

1. "8 Black-Capped Chickadee Calls EXPLAINED," posted September 2, 2018, by Lesley the Bird Nerd, YouTube, https://www.youtube.com/watch?v=reKoV7pD9CA.
2. "Why Do Some Birds Mimic the Sounds of Other Species?," All About Birds, Cornell Lab of Ornithology, accessed April 25, 2024, https://www.allaboutbirds.org /news/why-do-some-birds-mimic-the-sounds-of-other-species.

3. He placed birds in his creation for my pleasure and his praise.
The sounds of the birds, such as the peaceful cooing of a dove, call me to relax, be still, and praise the One who made them. If lyrics were put to their tune, I like to imagine they are crying out, "Glory! Glory! Glory!" or "See what God has done! See what God has done!" The extravagant intricacies of their songs call me to worship the One who made them to be what they are.

The birds invite me to make a choice. I can pursue more knowledge for myself. I can fret over what I can't hear or see. Or I can pause, enjoy the wonders of what I can see and hear, and praise the One who serves as composer, choreographer, and conductor of creation's orchestra, singing in praise of him.

He deserves every recitative of "Glory! Glory! Glory!"

Lord God, you are the One who put songs in the throats of birds. Thank you for the way their songs remind me of your power, majesty, and rule over all the earth.

·············· LISTENING WITH OPEN EARS ··············

The next time you hear a bird chorus, quietly slip outside, close your eyes, and listen carefully to the song. Create your own lyrics to match the music, and praise the God of creation.

7

Woodpeckers

*I will consider all your works and meditate on all
your your mighty deeds.*
PSALM 77:12

*M*y introduction to the woodpecker came on an early summer
morning at our home in North Carolina at 5:00 a.m. He perched
on the side of a tree trunk outside my bedroom window, drilling a rat-
a-tat-tat into the morning stillness.

I covered my head. It didn't smother the sound.

"What is that noise?" I asked my husband.

"It's a woodpecker," he said, annoyed. His disdain resurfaced years
later when we moved to Arizona and found that in the desert South-
west woodpeckers like to drill holes in the gutters, siding, and roofs
of homes. We took the necessary precautions to "woodpecker-proof"
the siding of our home, but my husband's surly comments continued.
Evidently, Jack has little use for woodpeckers.

I, however, was intrigued. Only hearing and never seeing our noisy
intruder, I wondered how the woodpecker could make such a far-
reaching drilling sound. I read that the noisy bird makes that sound
with his beak, not with vocal cords. Woodpeckers do have a select list
of calls, but they are more limited than other bird species. They use

their beaks to drum a rapid-fire mating call or warning system. The slower tapping sound happens when they drill holes into trees—and houses—to find insects for food or to create nests, which they later abandon for other critters to use.

Surely, you'd think, incessant drilling would give the poor dear a headache at best, a concussion at worst. But the connected, hard-as-iron skull and beak surround a precision cushion layer that stretches around the bird's brain. It is so ingeniously designed that engineers have modeled "black box" flight data recorders in airplanes as well as crash helmets after the woodpecker's skull.

But what causes the sound? The woodpecker's beak, of course. Right? Ah, but the woodpecker needs something to peck. Without wood—or houses—his peck would be the sound of silence. He needs the wood to make the sound.

That truth is simple and yet so profound. Think it through with me. God created everything in this world to work together in perfect sync. He made the woodpecker. He made the trees. He created sound and our ears. When the invisible vibration of the jabbing beak against the tree's bark travels through the air, the ears of all nature (including mine at 5:00 a.m.) catch the sound.

God made the individual parts to work together as a collective. He designed it all, and he maintains it all. He is ruler of it all.

God intended the church to work that way too. Paul made this connection in his letter to the Colossian church:

> [Christ] made the things we can see
>   and the things we can't see. . . .
> He holds all creation together.
> Christ is also the head of the church,
>   which is his body.
>   (Col. 1:16–18 NLT)

God made each of us to be individuals, with a unique combination of skills, spiritual gifts, and experiences that make us one of a kind. He designed the church to consist of separate, unique, and complex parts that work in tandem with each other so they can establish his kingdom on earth. Ephesians 4:16 says, "He makes the whole body fit together perfectly. As each part does its own special work, it helps the other parts grow, so that the whole body is healthy and growing and full of love" (NLT).

God created everything in this world to work together in perfect sync.

Have you ever wondered how certain people in your church will fit in with the others? Questioned how God could ever use those people to bless and build the body of Christ? I have. But to look at the woodpecker is to remember that God has a place for each person in his design and God makes no mistakes.

Why does the created world need woodpeckers? Surely other birds can catch insects and build nests without such noisy hammering. In a family discussion about the usefulness of woodpeckers, my sister answered this way: "Perhaps woodpeckers do what other birds can't do." How else would birds remove insects from trees? That's a job for a woodpecker!

God's extravagant creativity shows us that there's more than one way to catch a bug or accomplish a task. God used the woodpecker's schematics to provide blueprints for human pursuits, like black boxes and crash helmets. The woodpecker's peck becomes the percussion section of the avian orchestra, reminding us through its rat-a-tat-tat how creative God can be in the fitting together of all his creation.

In the same way, God's people work together, each one doing their part to add to the whole. And when we make it possible for each person to fully do their special work, all of us benefit. When I do what I'm designed to do, I help the person next to me grow, and they do the same for me. That verse from Ephesians says we'll end up healthy and stronger. We'll actually love each other more when we allow ourselves to be what God made us to be.

God's people need you. And you need them, even the ones who don't seem to fit your church's profile, family dynamic, or community group. Each person is important. Each one has something to offer.

By working together, everyone doing what they do best, all of us are better prepared to proclaim God's word boldly, love sincerely, and endure courageously. We do it through the power of Christ who holds all creation together, using our gifts and fulfilling the different purposes God has given to each one of us—even if we feel as unique and noisy as a woodpecker.

> *Lord, thank you for designing the woodpecker. Thank you for this reminder of how you made all things in the world fit together. Help me work with those around me, using the special gifts you have given to me. Help me appreciate and encourage the special gifts you have given to those working with me.*

LISTENING WITH OPEN EARS

What other parts of creation work together in perfect rhythm? Like the example of woodpeckers, songbirds, and sound, break down a system within nature or within the human anatomy into individual parts. Thank God for his perfect design of each part and how he expertly fits them together to work as one.

8

Barking Dogs

I love the LORD, for he heard my voice;
he heard my cry for mercy.
PSALM 116:1

A neighbor stopped me on the street. "Um . . ." She paused and jerked a thumb toward our house. "Your dog . . ."

Uh oh, I thought. *What has Riley done now?*

She shifted her feet. "When you all leave . . . well . . . he howls."

Not my dearly beloved Labrador retriever. This was the happy dog we could badger into conversations. We'd egg him on. "What do you want, Riley?"

Woof.

"Tell us about it, Riley."

Woof, woof.

His tail would lash the doorframe, and his ears would flop forward with each exuberant bark. Hearing us laugh elicited a series of yips that made us laugh harder.

This is why I don't own fish. You can't talk with fish.

Riley, unhappy? Say it isn't so. But Jack and I went for a walk one day and snuck behind a tree. Sure enough, loud, forlorn wails emitted from the house. We would've laughed harder if it hadn't been so pathetic.

Dogs and other domesticated animals carry within them a set of voices that express their needs and reactions. A herding dog by nature, the Welsh corgi we once owned was expert at vocalizing a series of quiet woofs when she thought I needed to be somewhere I wasn't. During my childhood, our family's German shepherd would stand in the shadows of our back yard and utter nothing more than a low growl at an intruder in the alley behind our home. It was menacing enough to make anyone flee. And then there are the neighborhood dogs that think they're the official town criers and alert their humans to anything happening outside. We're never sure of their intent: warning, greeting, or the bored need to find something to yap at.

God gave dogs, cats, horses, birds, and other domesticated animals these limited "voices" so they could express their intentions, needs, and reactions to people. It's a binary level of communication, far removed from our complexity of language, but it gets the job done. As humans, we interpolate what the animals mean, even though they haven't articulated it in so many words.

I've had times when my house animals were vocal, and in frustration, I've said, "I don't know what you want." Imagine what life would be like if they couldn't express themselves at all. Our interactions with them would be more confusing and less secure—and certainly not as much fun!

People have a vast advantage over animals in our ability to use language, reasoning, and emotion. (Although, after hearing Riley's howls, lack of emotion in animals might be debatable.) If that disparity exists between animals and humans, think about the gulf that lies between God and us. We are finite beings; he is infinite, not bound by time and space. We speak within the confines of one or a few languages; he knows and discerns the thoughts and attitudes of the heart (Heb. 4:12) and has invisible qualities that shout his character to the whole earth (Rom. 1:20).

I may not understand fully what my dog is trying to tell me, but God understands my clumsy cry. He has put his Holy Spirit within believers so that when we try to tell God in our imperfect way what we want, "the Spirit himself intercedes for us through wordless groans"

(Rom. 8:26)—groans that God understands. God not only hears our limited vocabulary; he knows what resides within our hearts before we attempt to tell him. The Spirit connects our desires with the will of God and acts as our interpreter and emissary (see v. 27).

> We speak within the confines of one or a few languages; God knows the thoughts and attitudes of the heart.

I'm so glad God hears my voice and understands what I'm trying to say. Like my desire to nurture my woebegone Labrador, the Lord wants to nurture me and bring me into a state of rest and contentment. But unlike my inability to understand exactly what to do for my dog, God knows how to give me so much more than what I think I need. With mercy I don't deserve, he provides everything according to his best plan for me. And in happy moments when I stumble over myself, he's probably smiling, but he'll never laugh at me. "Tell me more," he'll say, and we'll share the moment of delight together as I bask in his presence while sharing myself with him.

I love you, Lord!

Thank you, Lord, for giving voices to our domesticated animals and for the pleasure it gives us to interact with them and care for them as you've asked us to do. Thank you for your unlimited ability to understand what I try to say to you and for always responding with love and mercy.

LISTENING WITH OPEN EARS

Listen to an animal in your house or a neighbor's yard. How many types of barks or sounds can you catalog? Thank God for his creative design as heard in the voices of the animals around you.

9

Voices

My sheep listen to my voice; I know them,
and they follow me.
JOHN 10:27

The first time I saw my future husband across a crowded auditorium, I was not impressed. In the years before my Better Than Ever vision, most things were blurry blobs, and there was nothing exciting about that blurry blob.

Then I heard his voice. And I fell. Hard. It was a rich, deep bass voice: articulate, resonant, intellectual, and confident. He sounded like he knew what he was talking about. Today, years later, that aspect sometimes drives me crazy. But back then, I was smitten. I wanted to know this person.

The human voice is a marvelous creation. It is the starting point of sounds organized into words and language, the basis of our interactions with each other. And it isn't only the words we utter that communicate, for our mouths add layers of inflection, volume, and emotion. We can manipulate meaning by the ways we stress or pause over certain words. We can masquerade our identities by flexing our intonation into other voices.

Beyond that, each voice is distinct, as one-of-a-kind as a fingerprint.

Voices are so customized that I can walk into a crowded room today and immediately pick out the sound of my beloved—and swoon all over again.

This ability to communicate shows that we bear the image of God. We are the only part of God's creation that has words, language, thoughts, and emotion at our disposal, just like God does. It makes me wonder if God gave us vocal cords and language so he could communicate with us in ways we could understand. God makes clear in the pages of Scripture that he longs to have a relationship with us and makes it possible for us to know him.

As I see and hear God's creation and read of his great deeds on my behalf, I long to become more attuned to his voice than any other; for his words express who he is and what is important to him. But is it possible for my heavenly Father's voice to become as familiar, as beloved, as my husband's distinctive tones? Yes! Jesus once compared our relationship with God to a flock of sheep that respond readily to a shepherd's voice: "When he has brought out all his own, he goes on ahead of them, and his sheep follow him because they know his voice" (John 10:4).

I long to become more attuned to God's voice than any other.

Today, God communicates through the pages of his Word and the thoughts of our minds as guided by his Holy Spirit. But how can we distinguish our Father's voice from all the other "voices" in the world that compete for our attention and agreement?

Just as I learned to distinguish the voice of my husband, we become acquainted with the voice of God by spending time with him. Reading and studying his Word reveals what he is like and what matters to him. The more we apply and practice what he's told us, the closer we'll move toward him. Our hearts and spirits will crave that close relationship he invites us to have, and we'll find ourselves turning more and more to his Word. We'll seek the Word, not because we have to, not merely because we know it's a healthy practice, but because we want to, because we crave it. God's words will become "sweeter than honey" (Ps. 19:10), causing us to swoon with delight.

I have a long way to go in my relationship with Jesus. Only in the last few years have I experienced that "sweeter than honey" sensation when I read the Bible. But I find myself feeling increasing delight over certain Bible passages. I'll read verses like "I love you, LORD, my strength. The LORD is my rock, my fortress and my deliverer; my God is my rock, in whom I take refuge, my shield and the horn of my salvation, my stronghold" (Ps. 18:1–2) and I'll linger over each phrase, thinking of all the ways God has been my rock and my fortress, remembering wonderful times when my family saw his sustaining power. I'll smile with the memory, blink twice, and lean in to read more.

Today, fall in love with the voice of Jesus. Learn to recognize it. Pay attention to what he says in his Word, what you see him doing in the world, and how he prompts you to move forward through his Holy Spirit. The more we apply and practice what he has told us, the closer we move toward him, the more familiar his words and ways become. As his voice becomes more distinct and delightful, the chatter of the earth will diminish.

When you hear his voice, you will smile; for you have become familiar with his voice, and his voice will bring you joy.

Father, thank you for creating the complexities of the human voice that fill us with contentment and joy. Thank you that you offer us that kind of familiarity and intimacy with yourself. I want your voice to be more important and detectable to me than any human voice in my life. Show me how I can become more familiar with all your ways.

LISTENING WITH OPEN EARS

Set aside extra time this week to spend with God and his Word. Tell the Lord you want to know him better. Write a list of what you learn about God in the time you spend with him.

Babies

But Jesus called the children to him and said,
"Let the little children come to me, and do not
hinder them, for the kingdom of God belongs
to such as these."

LUKE 18:16

*R*ight in the middle of a worship service, my three-year-old had a full-blown meltdown. Despite my preacher husband's insistence that crying babies don't distract him from preaching, I figured this tantrum was sure to challenge that resolve. Of greater concern, I feared it would bother others. It certainly was bothering me. I tried to console and redirect, but her screams only intensified.

In desperation, I carried the writhing child out of the auditorium, certain that disapproving eyes were dogging my every step. One woman got up and followed me. *Oh dear*, I thought, *here it comes. My kid is ruining your worship experience.*

In the hallway, the woman held open her arms. "Let me take her for you."

"We've got this," I told her. Never let it be said that the minister's wife couldn't get her toddler under control.

"Listen, Karen," she replied. "Once in a while, every parent needs a break from their children, and children need a break from their parents. You go back in and enjoy the service." She took my daughter, who immediately settled in her arms.

I appreciate what my wise friend did. But I was embarrassed, anticipating my husband's rebuke for the disturbance. "Did you hear what happened?" I asked later.

"No, what?" He had missed it all. And in that moment, he reaffirmed his stance on crying babies in worship services. "It's the sound of life and hope. Babies are the future for a church."

An hour-long, adult-focused worship service is a tough environment for a little one who doesn't have the skills to sit and listen. Babies have needs that divide the parent's attention. I appreciate churches that provide excellent childcare so parents can devote their entire attention to meeting their own spiritual needs. But every parent knows there are unavoidable moments when baby needs to be with mama. And babies cry—whether in church, on an airplane, or at Walmart on a Friday night. And moms and dads worry that the crying will annoy someone.

For many of us, the crying isn't bothersome. Jack is right. Crying *is* the sound of life, hope, innocence, and our future. God created babies to cry.

Jesus showed his perspective on children when some moms wanted him to bless their little ones. But his disciples wanted to stick with the program and send away the distraction. In their culture, children were on the lower end of the social scale. It was thought best for them not to be seen or heard during the important work of teaching and healing. Jesus disagreed. He used the interruption as a teachable moment, holding up children as an example of the type of person who belongs in God's kingdom.

Later, after Jesus's triumphal procession into Jerusalem, some children got rowdy in the temple courts. To the Jewish leaders, though, the children's noisy voices weren't the problem. It was the words within the shouts that pushed their indignation button: "Hosanna to the Son of David" (Matt. 21:15). These uneducated children were calling this imposter the Messiah! When they questioned Jesus about it, he quoted Psalm 8:2, which says that God has called forth praise from the mouths of infants and children.

> Babies' crying *is* the sound of life, hope, innocence, and our future. God created babies to cry.

How much did Jesus value the children? Enough to carve time from his ministry schedule to hold and bless them. Enough to champion them for their expressions of praise. Enough to call them to him and say, I imagine, with a smile on his face and a crook of his finger, "Come here."

Why?

Because the low social status, innocence, and simple dependence of children can teach the adults in the crowd a lot about life in God's kingdom. In their simple, unfiltered minds, children don't restrain themselves or give second thoughts to praising God in places and at times the adults might call inappropriate. Children have value. Children have lots to offer the adults in the room. Every child. Born or unborn.

In those moments when I refuse to recognize a child's presence or when I find fault with their exuberance and interruptions, I fall into the role of Jesus's self-appointed public relations experts. But Jesus calls me to live what I say I believe. If I champion the preservation of an unborn child, I also need to show respect, devotion, and care for the child crying in front of me.

The cry of a baby calls us to remember that God values life—every season of it. Children are worth delaying an adult conversation so we can get down on their level and exclaim over what they want to show us. They are worth our sacrifice of time or personal pursuits. They are also worth our investment of time in keeping our marriages strong and in building and strengthening our own relationships with God so they have examples to follow. They are worth keeping close in our hugs and hearts. For one day, they will fly the nest and no longer be within arm's reach.

All children. Grandchildren. Nieces and nephews. The babies in the church nursery and the ones in the auditorium. The cute babies with glittered bows and the somber ones with marks of abuse done behind closed doors. God loves them all and so should we.

Even when they cry. Especially when they cry.

Thank you, God, for giving babies the ability to cry, for their cry reminds me how Jesus valued children. Help me follow his example by providing an unhindered path to your open arms and cherishing them as you do.

LISTENING WITH OPEN EARS

Ask God to connect you with a child this week. Intentionally take the time to notice the child and interact with them. Thank God that the child before you is important to him.

11

Laughter

A cheerful heart is good medicine.

PROVERBS 17:22

I loved visiting my ear, nose, and throat doctor. It wasn't the doctor, necessarily. It was something about the office. There was an ambience I couldn't quite define. It took me several visits to figure out what made the place distinctive from other medical facilities.

What was it?

They laughed.

The receptionist greeted me each time with a smile, called me by name, and bantered easily. As I sat in the waiting room, I heard staff in the background laughing with each other. Once, during a minor procedure on my nose, the doctor and his assistant kept up a running stream of one-liners and jokes, then reprimanded me for not holding still. *Then stop being so funny*, I thought. *No, wait! Don't stop.*

Their good humor made such a difference in my visits for earaches and sinus infections. I've been to medical offices—and I suppose you have too—where I could feel the tension. Techs talked like they were reading a script. Receptionists and financial personnel doled out cold-hearted rebuttals to people's reasons for missing an appointment or not producing proper documentation. And they passed each other like ships in the night, harried, hassled, and overworked. You can hardly blame them for being out of sorts.

But my ENT's office showed that laughter is not off-limits in a medical facility. In fact, it's actually a very good idea. It heals minds and bodies, moods and relationships. Everything runs more smoothly with a bit of laughter and a kind word.

God is the author of joy. He created us with the capacity to feel joy even amid tough times. He put within each of us the ability to experience pleasure through the sound of laughter and the sight of a smile.

I don't know what made that medical group so zany happy. But I do know that as Christians, we have lots to laugh about—not in derision or mocking people for their failures but delighting over what we see God doing. When Abraham and Sarah had a child after decades of barrenness, they responded to his miraculous birth by naming him Isaac, which means "laughter." Sarah said, "God has brought me laughter, and everyone who hears about this will laugh with me" (Gen. 21:6). Sarah had every reason to laugh with delight at her son's birth. God had done an incredible, amazing thing, something she had long resigned herself to believing would never happen. But it did! Finally, beyond all reasonable hope, she got the desire of her heart—a baby. Delight doesn't begin to describe the joy she must have felt!

God is the author of joy.

God created us to feel pleasure. He put within us the emotions to express joy and pleasure through laughter. And he gave us this gift to bring healing to our souls and to bless and nurture the lives of those around us. A cheerful heart—or in the case of my doctor's office, several cheerful hearts—*is* good medicine.

Best of all, God has given us plenty to laugh about. Think of the incredible, unlikely things you have seen him do. Healing what doctors said couldn't be healed. Providing the money, groceries, or clothes you needed when you hadn't told anyone except the Lord about your specific needs. Watching your work bring results over which you had no control, knowing it was obviously God's doing.

Think of the stories you've heard about people coming to faith in Christ by the droves. I can't help but smile when I think about the mass baptism that happened at Pirate's Cove, California, in 2023.[3] Four thousand baptized in one day! What else have you heard? What else is God doing in the world? It's enough to open our mouths with a smile so the laughter of surprise and delight bubbles forth. "Look what God did this time!"

When we focus on God's goodness, love, and power, we have the salve of joy that soothes our wounds and renews our strength; in fact, his joy is our strength (Neh. 8:10). We can share a consistently joyful spirit with others because we're confident that no matter how bad life gets, God is good. He is creator of all that is good, and in the end, *he will win*.

So, good job ENT doctor's office staff. You made me smile and relax. That, in itself, spurred on healing. And you motivated me to take laughter with me when I left your clinic. When we're empowered like this, with faith and confidence in God's goodness, we can find an extra special dose of joy, knowing that laughter, pleasant words, and cheerful hearts are gifts straight from the Father's hand.

Dear Father God, thank you for creating the sound of laughter. Thank you for designing us to feel pleasure and share delight through cheerful words and good laughs. Most of all, thank you for the gift of joy!

·········· LISTENING WITH OPEN EARS ··········

Listen for a good laugh today, one that is uninhibited and full of delight. Don't hear any? What makes you laugh with delight? Do it— and share the joy with someone else.

---

3. Talia Wise, "'The Biggest Water Baptism' in US History? 4,166 Baptized at Historic Beach from Jesus Movement," CBN, May 31, 2023, https://.cbn.com/news/us/biggest-water-baptism-us-history-4166-baptized-historic-beach-jesus-movement.

12

Crickets

But Jesus replied, "My Father is always
working, and so am I."
JOHN 5:17 NLT

The noise of the day had ceased, and I lay in bed, waiting for sleep to come. I spent those last few moments of the day in prayer, bringing names and situations I cared about before God's throne of grace, attempting to surrender my concerns into his capable hands.

My brain hit the pause button after the last item on my list. And I heard . . . crickets.

The new slang meaning for the word *crickets* amuses me. If you aren't familiar with this term, it's used to signify "nothing." In other words, someone expects a response from someone else and it isn't forthcoming—no answer at all, nothing. All activity has ceased, no one has anything to say. It's so quiet that the only noise is like the background consistency of a cricket's chirp.

Your spouse doesn't answer your texts—"Crickets!" A newscaster asks a question, and the official refuses to answer—"Crickets!" An actor performs and the audience fails to applaud, leaving the space so quiet you can hear that pesky cricket that crawled through a crack in the stage door. We've all had moments when we've tried to reach someone but got no response. The solution? Expel your frustration with one word: "Crickets!"

The poor cricket.

From the bug's point of view, "nothing" is not what's happening. That little insect is belting out its melody in the way the Creator made it to do so. If it could think like a human, that cricket might retort, "What am I—nothing? I'm working, I'm working."

And so is Jesus.

In my late-night prayers, anxiety and impatience over my requests can keep me from falling asleep. After all, I've often been praying the same prayers for days, weeks. And nothing has happened. God seems silent. All I hear is crickets.

Crickets.

I *do* hear crickets—real crickets outside my bedroom window. They are not silent. They offer a sweet, calming, peace-filled sound, the sound God put in place to lull me to sleep, reminding me with every chirp that I can do so in peace because he never sleeps. "Indeed, he who watches over Israel will neither slumber nor sleep" (Ps. 121:4).

And yet my waiting moments remain silent. No answers. No soft reassurances.

Anyone who has been part of a planning team for a large project or production knows that a successful program is 15 percent brilliance and 85 percent hard, tedious work. The public eye sees only the finished product, but those who've labored to make it happen know it has taken months, even years, working in private to set everything in place and make that final magical moment happen.

Yet, somehow, we expect God to do all things in an instant, to bring immediate resolution or snap his divine fingers and make everything okay right now. Instead, if we quiet our inner turmoil and listen closely, we hear the soft rhythmic sounds that assure us much *is* happening—not on the stage of our public life but behind the scenes, where God is setting everything in place. After all, God took six days to create the world. Jesus lived for thirty years on this earth before beginning a three-year ministry that culminated in the great work of the cross and resurrection. And Lazarus lay in a grave four days before his decaying body was brought back to life, proving with no doubt that Jesus was Lord over life and death (see John 11).

> ## If we quiet our inner turmoil and listen closely, we hear the soft rhythmic sounds that assure us much *is* happening behind the scenes.

God is not slow to answer. He is not late bringing about the fulfillment of his promises. Instead, he invites us to use this quiet period to grow stronger, cultivate our relationship with him, and find peaceful rest so we can be ready for the God-sized answer he plans to give. And he sprinkles clues of his work around us, like peaceful night sounds. If we lean in close, we can hear him at work and see his progress.

Have you prayed long and hard for something and wondered why you hear only silence? Listen again. Pay attention. Do you hear the sound of crickets? Let their soft, constant chirp remind you that while you might not see God's progress on your request, God is backstage, building his masterpiece. He's heard you, he knows what you need, and he's at work to bring you his best.

Lord God, in faith, I accept that you are working to bring about the fulfillment of your purposes and promises, even when I can't see or hear it. Thank you for the reminder you give through the peaceful, consistent sound of a cricket's chirp that you are always at work for my benefit.

LISTENING WITH OPEN EARS

The next time you hear a cricket, listen to its chirp. Use the sound to remind you to thank God that he has heard your prayers and he's at work even while you fall asleep.

13

Night Owls

In peace I will lie down and sleep, for you alone,
LORD, make me dwell in safety.
PSALM 4:8

*F*inished with my prayer list and lulled into peace by the rhythmic chirp of our resident cricket, I entered the antechamber of my night's sleep, only to be jerked awake by a lone "Hoot!" I sighed and tried again.

"Hoo-hoot!"

"Did you hear that pesky owl outside our bedroom window last night?" I asked my husband as I rubbed my bleary eyes the next morning. "He was so noisy. And did you hear what the neighbors said? Owls are nasty things. There was even a warning about keeping an extra eye on cats and small dogs late at night because the owls will get them."

Jack paused before answering. "I find the call rather soothing."

Time to regroup.

I've long learned that misunderstanding and ignorance breed annoyance, so I decided to learn more about my noisy intruder. I discovered that only one species of owl, the great horned owl, will attack cats and small dogs under nine pounds, and that's usually when the owl's territory is threatened. They are far more interested in a nighttime snack of rodents, insects, and—phew—an occasional skunk.

Other than that, they are fascinating creatures. One of the few animals with binocular vision, they don't need those long-distance laser eyes in the back of their heads because their neck muscles are more limber than a world-champion gymnast. While the rest of the world sleeps, they go on pest patrol and act as nighttime security guards, giving their occasional hoot to let insomniacs know they're keeping the world safe and secure from the latest insect invasion.

Owls have their place in the world. They do the job God has given to them well.

In fact, think of this. God crafted nighttime sounds to be different from daytime chatter. There are fewer animal sounds, but also, the sounds are lower pitched and slower in tempo. The nature noises you hear at night are the peaceful sounds of crickets, hoot owls, and the occasional bullfrog's grunt. Never mind the half-crazed rooster who woke up in the wrong time zone.

Creation works that way because God made it that way. He intended to slow the rhythms of life so that we, his highest creation, might find rest. And the hoot owl perching in a nearby tree sings a lullaby of God's watchful care over us.

Oh yes, he does watch over us. His mind never slips away from us. "He will not let your foot slip—he who watches over you will not slumber; indeed, he who watches over Israel will neither slumber nor sleep" (Ps. 121:3–4). His gifts are good, meant to bless and benefit us and remind us of his good will toward us (see James 1:17). If God made it, it's good—all creation is good.

The hoot owl perching in a nearby tree sings a lullaby of God's watchful care.

So instead of feeling hypersensitive about the hoot of a lone night owl, I have learned to make use of nature's nighttime benediction as a prompt to praise God for all his good gifts. I have started to end my nightly prayers in thanks for what God has given me.

A cooled house, safe from summer's heat.

The man next to me who, with one comment, recalibrated my attitude toward God's creation.

Good work throughout the day that makes me ready for sleep.

The sounds of creation that speak of God's character—his power, love, wisdom, extravagant creativity, perfection, and precision.

God's grace and mercy as expressed through Jesus's death on the cross.

The peace, joy, contentment, and transformed life I experience when I yield myself to his righteous ways.

And even a lone hoot owl that, in the last hour of the night, calls me to ponder what I hear and to listen for the sound of my heavenly Father's voice.

Hoot! Peace. Praise. All is well. Sleep.

Thank you, Lord, for the sounds of creation and how they invite me to draw closer to you. Thank you for this reminder that I can rest well, knowing that you are in control and all creation is working as it should.

LISTENING WITH OPEN EARS

Do you hear the voice of an owl where you live? Let that sound or another nightly nature sound prompt you to consider and recount the gifts God has given you throughout your day.

PART TWO

SOUND HEARING
How We Hear

14

Household Hums

*Be still and know that I am God; I will be exalted
among the nations, I will be exalted in the earth.*

PSALM 46:10

*I*t can happen day or night. A tornado, ice storm, lightning strike, downed power line, transformer explosion—any of these can throw the next few moments or hours into silence.

You've lost electric power.

In response, you open curtains to let in daylight, grabbing a flashlight or matches to light candles so you can fill in the dark spaces. But something is still missing. The normal household hums are absent: the drone of the refrigerator, computer, ceiling fans, air-conditioning and heating units, even the low hum emanating from a charger. Everything else seems loud: footsteps, doors shutting, or the rush of wind outside. You temper your voice, realizing how much noise layers our everyday moments and how you subconsciously talk over the hum.

Loss of electricity can be frustrating and inconvenient, but it can also be liberating; until then, you haven't realized the extra effort it takes to hear and be heard. You become acutely aware of the number and variety of noises we hear simultaneously.

God created our ears to hear in layers. Much as our eyes can grasp multiple details in one glance, our ears hear dozens of sounds at once, and our brains categorize those sounds within a nanosecond, with minimal effort or awareness from us. So used to tuning out the everyday hums, we add more and more noises to our life sphere. It takes an act of nature at the breaker box to make us realize how much we've masked the more important voices.

God turned down the noise in Elijah's life so the overworked prophet could rest, regroup, and clearly hear God's strategy for his next assignment. After proving that God was the one and only God at Mount Carmel and working with God to bring rain after a three-year drought, Elijah fled from Queen Jezebel's vengeful wrath and collapsed in a cave, so distressed that he prayed for death. God let Elijah sleep and eat before calling him to the mouth of the cave. The noisy sounds of a rock-smashing windstorm, an earthquake, and a fire passed by Elijah, forces of nature any of us would fear. But God wasn't part of those scary events. Instead, God turned off nature's noise and spoke with a gentle whisper. Elijah covered his face in worship, for he recognized this as the voice of God (1 Kings 19:12–13). God spoke, Elijah listened, and Elijah obeyed.

When we step away from the things that frighten or distract us, we're better able to hear the voice of God, to "be still, and know that [he is] God" (Ps. 46:10). We learn that God's gentle whisper carries more clout than the noisiest nature sounds or the most deafening roar of human-made power.

> When we step away from the things
> that frighten or distract us, we're better
> able to hear the voice of God.

It takes discernment to know which noises we need to turn down. It isn't as simple as shutting off a ceiling fan; it takes intentionality to categorize the sounds that currently fill our lives and choose what God would have us hear. We might have to get creative to make space for ourselves. We may need to erect a barrier to those sounds that threaten to pull us away from God. We may get up a few minutes early or tell those we love that we need a moment by ourselves so we can spend time with God alone. We may need to reroute our thoughts back to God ten times over as our mind drifts from our prayer list.

Turning off or tuning out the noise takes persistence and discipline. But it's worth it. It's worth hearing God's gentle voice and reconnecting with him in the quiet. For when we listen in the silence, we listen without distraction. Our ears and minds don't strain to hear the sounds on the edge of our subconscious. God has our full attention, and we don't miss his words.

When the power comes back on, and we return to daily life, we may find we miss the quiet. But in the process of defining the sounds in our lives, we can rediscover what noises enter our ear canal and realize we have a choice about what we listen to. Knowing it's a choice and finding delight in the stillness make us long for those sweet moments when the sound of the important becomes more distinct.

You won't be able to turn all of it off. Instead, praise God that you can hear so much at one time. Then make time in your day to retreat to a quieter sector so you can focus on what God wants you to hear in that moment.

Thank you, Father, for giving me the incredible ability to hear many things at one time. Guide me to be discerning about what noises I listen to and what unnecessary noises I'm adding to my life that keep me from hearing what you want me to hear.

LISTENING WITH OPEN EARS

Retreat for a few moments to a quiet place. What sounds are missing? What sounds do you hear? Use those few moments to have an uninterrupted conversation with your heavenly Father.

15

Horse Hooves

Great is the LORD and most worthy of praise; his
greatness no one can fathom.
PSALM 145:3

When my children were young, my grandfather paid for the entire family to spend a week at a dude ranch in Colorado. This particular ranch was known for its daily horse-riding expeditions. I was both excited and nervous. I had always wanted to ride a horse. But with my limited vision, could I?

Of more concern, would the ranch's riding instructor prevent me from riding once she heard I couldn't see? After all, I was the girl my high school athletic director expelled from the physical education department because she feared I would fall on the track and hold the school liable.

But the riding instructor took my limited vision in stride. "You don't need to see to ride a horse," she said. "You can identify the terrain by what you hear and what you feel through your horse."

How awesome! I quickly distinguished the sounds my horse made as he walked through crunching gravel, hard-packed dirt, and high grass. I heard the change in rhythm as he shifted his weight over boulders, slowed to catch a grass snack on the side of the road, or picked up his pace as we neared the barn at the end of a ride. I could hear and feel changes on inclines and declines, and I learned to shift in sync with his course corrections. It was as if my horse became an extension of my own body, and he did the seeing for me.

Every day that week, I found myself eager to discover other nuances of sound. How else would one element of nature combine with another to produce an exponential array of possibilities? What variables had to happen to make one basic sound change? And what other information about my world could I gather from the way sound waves entered my ear canals? From years of legal blindness, I already knew how to depend on my hearing, but a week with a horse named General opened a world of complex, intricate sounds I had not bothered to explore, appreciate, or use.

"Oh, the depth of the riches of the wisdom and knowledge of God! How unsearchable his judgments, and his paths beyond tracing out!" says Romans 11:33. The nature of God is far more elaborate than the complexity of sound made by a horse's hooves. Yet I've tended to generalize God's character. I've devised baseline definitions for terms like mercy, grace, righteousness, and love, and then gone on my merry way through life, thinking I understood God.

But the character of God offers a lifetime of exploration: the nuances of his forgiveness, the variegated colors of his grace, and the unlimited, creative ways he provides for each of us. Grace is one thing. Power is another. Grace plus power? Infinite combinations of expression! Displays of his power and glory are like treasures showcased in a huge exhibit hall far larger than the Smithsonian or the Louvre, available to explore and experience at no cost.

I may love my family members very much. I say I would do anything for them. Yet in my limited humanness, I can't do all that I want to do. I cannot save them from sickness or harm. But God has both power and love. He can do all that he wants to do for us. Conversely, he has unlimited power, yet he will always use his power for our best interests. His power is tempered by his love and compassion for us. The

God who can create and destroy worlds with a flick of his divine finger holds and preserves me in the strength of his hand because he loves me. I can hardly wrap my limited brain cells around the idea of a God that powerful and that loving. Yet he is.

The character of God offers a lifetime of exploration: the nuances of his forgiveness, the variegated colors of his grace, and the unlimited, creative ways he provides for each of us.

We'll never understand everything there is to know about God. Yet the more we understand, the more we can use that knowledge to move confidently through life and do what we thought was impossible—to live that Better Than Ever life that God has waiting for us. Understanding his righteousness teaches us how to be righteous. Experiencing his love shows us how to pass forward that love. And exploring the depths of his grace helps us realize the extraordinary freedom it gives us; that we don't have to earn our way into God's favor and we can drop our expectations of others. We learn through each experience that simple faith and trust in Jesus is enough.

My riding instructor taught me how to use my newfound knowledge to urge my horse into a canter across an open field. As we broke into a smooth rhythm, my body rose and fell in sync with General's pounding hooves. A line spoken by another neophyte rider filled my brain: *I raced the wind and I won!*

With each discovery about God's character, our lives become richer and fuller. We press forward, wanting to know more. Why? Because we've learned that when we allow our lives to connect with the wisdom of the Almighty and we discover how big and deep and wide is his love, we will push through the winds of this earth. And we will win.

*Father, I can never understand all there is to know about
you in this lifetime. Yet even the tiniest amount I can learn
about who you are will enrich my life beyond anything I
can possibly imagine. Thank you for being you.*

LISTENING WITH OPEN EARS

Choose a sound you hear every day. How many ways can that sound
change? Pause for a few moments to thank God for creating the structure of hearing to be so sophisticated.

16

Open Spaces

I will instruct you and teach you in the
way you should go; I will counsel you with
my loving eye on you.
PSALM 32:8

*A*s we stood in a covered walkway, my mobility instructor placed a blindfold over my eyes. "Now," she instructed, "walk forward. Let what you hear guide your steps. Tell me when you reach the parking lot."

My instructor had been contracted by the state's rehabilitation services to help me learn how to move through my world when I was sixteen years old. I didn't know the science behind bouncing sound waves; after all, I was the girl who refused to take high school physics because I feared it would ruin my grade point average. But as I walked forward that day, relying only on my hearing for navigation, I quickly discovered the difference in my perception of noises when I moved from that enclosed walkway into the wider area of the parking lot. Voices caught on the wind and became muffled. The open space introduced sounds of traffic and birds, previously blocked by the brick walls of the walkway.

The instructor took off my blindfold and concluded the lesson.

"When you walk at night or in unfamiliar territory, pay attention to how sound changes," she said. "It will help you know where you are." My new awareness dispelled my fears about walking by myself. The darkness of night didn't have to keep me from knowing where I was; listening for the interplay of sound waves would give me the information I needed to get where I wanted to go.

Being the curious person that I am, I later researched why noises sound different depending on where we are. I also learned why a singing group sounds so awesome in a cave. Sound waves have to go somewhere. In open spaces, they keep traveling, uninhibited. In an enclosed area, they keep bouncing off hard surfaces like out-of-control Ping-Pong balls, or they absorb into softer materials, allowing us to hear a clear, full sound. The way God created sound to interact with the environment is like markers on a hiking trail. Those differing sounds inform us about where we are and direct us toward where we need to go.

When I first became a Christ follower, I didn't understand how to do the Jesus thing. I didn't know where I was going or what I was doing. I knew I was saved by grace, but I wasn't clear on how that would affect my daily life and the choices I made each day. How would I hear God's voice? How would I know what God wanted me to do? How would I make sense of what his Word, the Bible, said?

I needed to listen. And I'm grateful God offers instruction in the way we should go (Ps. 32:8). For example, the Ten Commandments define a holy and blameless life. The list of character qualities in 1 Corinthians 13:4–7 expounds on God's brand of love. As we mature in our relationship with God, our understanding of how to obey and trust him increases, and we can figure out how to apply those over-arching doctrinal principles to everyday, real-life situations.

But I'm impatient. I want to know how I can hear God's voice better so I know what to do sooner. After all, I'm the girl who didn't want to ruin my grade point average by getting it wrong the first time out.

Jesus's parable of the sower helps me understand how I can more clearly absorb God's voice at the start. The story in Matthew 13:1–23 tells of a farmer who scattered his seed at planting season. Some seed fell on hard dirt and the birds quickly snatched it away. Other seed became choked by weeds and withered on rocky soil. The most successful seed fell on soft, absorbent soil that produced a good crop. If we want to hear God's directions and understand what he says in his Word, we need a soft, pliable, teachable spirit. We also need to remove those things that block our understanding or detract us from listening carefully. The ways of the world might seem harmless in and of themselves, but if we find certain things pulling us away from trusting God, that's a sign we may want to make some changes to our lifestyle.

> If we want to hear God's directions and understand what he says in his Word, we need a soft, pliable, teachable spirit.

When we've made the commitment to fully engage with God, he will lead us forward. We may not become oriented to the path right away, but thankfully, God gives lots of grace and teaches us through our failures as well as our successes. He will give us what we need for today if we ask for his guidance. And one day, we'll enter his throne room where the acoustics are out of this world, and we will hear his voice with perfect clarity.

Do you struggle with knowing how to live like Jesus wants you to live? Do you wonder what you should be doing next in your life? Ask the Lord to guide you. Admit you don't understand everything. Ask him to show you if you have a hardness of spirit or a wall of pride that causes his voice to bounce off the walls of your life. Assess the distractions that might be muffling what God wants you to know.

Keep praying, keep listening, and keep asking for discernment. Then step out in faith, trusting that God will guide you, step by step, into the realm of his perfect will.

Lord, understanding you and hearing you better is a growing process, and I'm willing to accept that. But I'm ready to make progress. I want to hear you better and understand what you have to say. Would you help me?

LISTENING WITH OPEN EARS

As we step forward in faith, we will better see, hear, and understand what God wants. Do you feel unsure of something you think God is asking you to do? Take the first step and then a second step, continuing to listen for his voice. Take notes of what you learn about God as you move forward.

17

Tour Guides

*In your unfailing love you will lead the people you
have redeemed. In your strength you will guide
them to your holy dwelling.*

EXODUS 15:13

$\mathcal{M}$y weeklong trip to Washington, DC, the summer before my high school senior year started on a disappointing note. We boarded a tour bus for an orientation to the capital city and the other students pressed their noses to the tinted windows, enthralled by the sights of the Capitol dome and the Lincoln Memorial. After five minutes, I slumped in my seat, frustrated that all I saw were bright lights and blurry blobs.

The tour guide was giving a running monologue, complete with historical and current trivia. Since I couldn't see anything, I started to listen and became engrossed in the details. Later that week, as we visited various sites in more depth, I blurted out some of the facts I'd heard. My friends' faces were as blank as a newly opened Word document. "Where did you hear that?"

I stared back. "Why, the tour guide Sunday night."

"We didn't hear him say that."

They were busy looking. I was busy listening.

I'm grateful the tour guide gave such an interesting presentation. Familiar with the layout of the city so we never made a wrong turn, he also knew an abundance of detail about what we saw and presented it in a lively manner that kept my attention. What more could I have wanted in a tour guide?

I wonder what that tour would have been like if someone who'd actually lived through that history had guided us? What if the first lady or president's chief of staff had boarded the bus? What if Dolley Madison told us of her efforts to save White House treasures from fire during the War of 1812? Or if the owner of Ford's Theatre described the night President Lincoln was shot? Those people had insider information. They would have been credible because they were there in those historical moments. I think my bus mates would have forgotten what was outside their windows as they listened to someone who had actually "been there, done that."

In the same way, we often wish for a tour guide through life, one with insider information. Wouldn't it be wonderful to have someone identify the circumstances we see coming toward us? Someone who hasn't merely read the information in a *Life For Dummies* book but who has actually gone through those life experiences? Someone who has "been there, done that"?

That would be Jesus.

The book of Hebrews tells us that Jesus became like us so he would be able to go before us, guiding us all the way—even navigating through death—to reach the eternal life he has planned for us (see Heb. 2:9).

What makes Jesus a worthy life guide?

As the source of all wisdom and truth, Jesus is fully trustworthy. We don't have to wonder if his facts or assessments are accurate. And unlike tour guides who are limited by their own lifespan, Jesus is the Alpha and Omega, the beginning and the end, the start of the past reaching to the end of the future.

Our Washington, DC, tour guide was just doing his job for yet another group of wide-eyed high school students. But God knows each of us by name. He's been everywhere. He's been intricately involved in every facet of human history. And he knows everything about us—how we're made, what we've been through, and what we fear. He knows everything about what's coming toward us, and he is fully capable of guiding us into our future. He does it all with unfailing love. He cares deeply about what is best for us. We can count on him to never lead us astray.

> Jesus became like us so he would be able to go before us, guiding us all the way—even navigating through death—to reach the eternal life he has planned for us.

Best of all, Jesus knows the way to walk through death into life. He knows from personal experience that God has the power to give life back to us, life that will last forever.

When it comes to matters of life and death, no other guide will do.

At one point in Jesus's ministry, the crowds became dissatisfied with his message and drifted away. Jesus turned to his disciples. "You do not want to leave too, do you?" he asked.

Peter answered him, "Lord, to whom shall we go? You have the words of eternal life" (John 6:68).

If I could have the tour guide of my dreams, I'd select someone with these qualifications—someone knowledgeable, with personal experience, and who's interested in me. Someone who cares that I reach my destination. Maybe even someone who knows me by name, who doesn't see me as just another face on the bus.

Likewise, if I could choose someone to guide me through this life, wouldn't I want someone who knows much more about life than I do—someone who won't lead me the wrong way? A person who looks out for my best interests and cares that I navigate well through life into heaven's best?

And if I found that perfect guide, wouldn't it be wise of me to listen?

Jesus is the best guide. He alone has the words of eternal life. Only he can lead us past earthly death and into the future of a forever life with God the Creator.

Let's listen to him.

Lord, you are the best guide through this earthly life. I trust you to lead me all the way to my heavenly home.

LISTENING WITH OPEN EARS

How have you seen God guide you this week? How has his guidance shown you that he is a credible, capable navigator of your life?

18

Sermons

When your words came, I ate them; they were my
joy and my heart's delight, for I bear your name,
LORD God Almighty.
JEREMIAH 15:16

When I was a child, I don't remember ever seeing my grandfather go to church. The family dismissed my question of "Why?" by saying Grandpa's profound hearing loss prohibited him from hearing much of the sermon and made music painful and distracting. But in later years, I overheard conversations between Grandpa and my uncle Ron, a preacher, that revealed a greater struggle. A consummate businessman, Grandpa wasn't about to buy into this Jesus stuff when the idea of God becoming man and dying on a cross didn't make sense.

Unknown to us, Grandpa was doing a lot of processing. Several weeks after another long discussion with Uncle Ron, who had left the house in utter frustration, my grandpa called him. "I think I get it and I'm ready," he said. At eight-six years old, he submitted his life to Christ through baptism. One aunt described her joy to me the day after: "My daddy, who used the name of Jesus as a curse word as long as I have known him, now proclaims him as Lord."

The surprises were still to come. Now Grandpa refused to let even hearing loss keep him from being in church every Sunday. Near the end of his life, he no longer had enough strength to participate in church, and in a visit with the pastor two days before his death, he said, "I'm sorry I let you down the last couple of weeks." He paused. "But I think I'm at the end of the trail."

Workers at his care home later told us that Grandpa wanted them to say the Lord's Prayer with him every night. They had to find a poster with the words and attach it to the wall to help the workers who didn't know it. But Grandpa remembered. He reached back into his childhood, where seeds of faith had been planted, and he used his memory of the Word to keep him connected with the Lord he now claimed.

I often think of Grandpa sitting in the worship center of that little church he and my mother attended, hardly able to hear anything the preacher said and enduring the discomfort of distorted music. Yet he was there because he wanted to be there. He found joy in being in the same room with other people who believed in Jesus. He got what he could out of the worship service even if it was nothing more than scraps of words.

I know about listening to sermons. I'm the wife of a retired pastor. I've heard the jokes about long sermons, the ones that put pew sitters to sleep, or the hard-hitting discourses that make listeners want to wear their steel-toed boots the following Sunday. I've heard twenty-minute messages that were still too long. You're probably thinking, *You really think a sermon can bring joy? Are you serious?*

Yes, I'm serious.

How can we find joy in listening to a thirty-minute or longer sermon without letting our minds wander or looking at our smart-phones? Thinking about Grandpa prompts the answer. If he was able to find joy in scraps, my satisfaction should burst out like a geyser simply because I can hear every precious word of truth and life.

What brings us joy in the hearing of God's Word? If we can hear the sermon without struggle, we are blessed. If we have a church we

can attend and our government allows us to go, or if our church group
has a working sound system, we are even more blessed.

Then there's the content of the message we hear, an easy-to-
understand gospel—even if it takes years for it to reach us or for us
to accept it. Think of the new believers in the book of Acts who heard
the good news about Jesus for the first time. When persecution hit the
young church in Jerusalem, a believer named Philip traveled to the
neighboring state of Samaria and started preaching. Acts 8:6–9 records
how the crowds paid close attention to what he said and that there "was
great joy in that city."

You really think a sermon can bring joy?
Are you serious? Yes, I'm serious.

The account of Paul's preaching in Philippi tells of a similar joyful
reaction. The jailer responsible for locking Paul and Silas in prison
feared for his life when an earthquake broke open the prison doors.
He figured he would be executed for letting prisoners escape, but Paul
reassured him that they were all there. Then Paul told him about Jesus,
and the Bible says the jailer "was filled with joy because he had come
to believe in God" (Acts 16:34).

We can find joy in hearing the message because it offers release and
so much more: life, peace, love, forgiveness, a second chance, hope,
and the promise of something absolutely wonderful after death. Like
the Samaritans and the Philippian jailer, our joy overflows when we
realize Jesus died on the cross to pay sin's price for us personally. Whoever we are, whatever we've done, and however long it has taken for us
to "get it," God wants us with him.

Even if we can hear only a little bit of God's life-saving message, it's
enough to bring us into God's ever-widening circle of those who have
entrusted their future to him. God invites us to find joy in what we
hear and move forward with what we understand.

The reason is simple: hearing is a privilege, and the Word of God is a gift.

Lord, thank you for ears to hear the words spoken by your messengers. Increase my joy that I can hear and understand the explanation of your Word and your ways.

·········· LISTENING WITH OPEN EARS ··········

Sunday's coming. Thank God that he has given you the privilege to hear and understand what will be said. Thank him for the messenger he has sent to share that word with you.

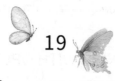

19

Longing to Belong

Carry each other's burdens, and in this way you
will fulfill the law of Christ.
GALATIANS 6:2

*W*henever Grandpa couldn't hear us, he'd say, "Hmm?" He always
said it with a certain tone of voice, one that had a soft edge when
he spoke to his grandkids but a harsher sound when he responded to
Grandma. And Grandma would answer loudly in a voice that sounded
equally annoyed and harsh to my young, inexperienced ears.

Now my husband, my soulmate, is losing his hearing. His favorite way to inform me is to say, "Can't hear you." I get annoyed. *Can*
you say that a little nicer, like with the same tone of affection Grandpa
would use with the grandchildren? And I raise my voice, sounding all
too much like my grandma.

"I'm not the problem," I told him once.

"I'm not frustrated at you," he replied in a moment of vulnerability.
"I'm frustrated at myself."

I, of all people, with my lifelong visual limits, should understand
his frustration. I've been there. I'm familiar with the emotions now
shared by my husband. Angst that we're not keeping up despite our
best efforts. Embarrassment that we might look weak and inferior.

Trepidation that someone in the crowd will suddenly doubt all our abilities if we admit to having trouble with one small detail. Or that they will judge us as being a complaining, lazy dependent, when the truth is that seeing or hearing takes at least twice as much effort for us as it does for the normally sighted or hearing person. And we are weary of the struggle. We wish someone would understand that we have days when we're tired of trying so hard to see or hear.

"You dropped your voice," Jack sometimes tells me. "You turned away. Come closer."

Why don't you move closer, dude? Why don't you put in your hearing aids? Why should I have to do the work of making it possible for you to hear?

Why not?

In his command "Do to others as you would have them do to you" (Luke 6:31), Jesus asks us to consider how we would like others to treat us. My own answer comes quickly: with compassion laced with dignity. *Include me. Accept me. Don't dismiss me.* I don't want to have to guess at the blurry outlines of my world alone. When I'm tired or overwhelmed, I don't want others to take over, but I sure would appreciate someone shouldering some of the burden or at least acknowledging that some life moments are more difficult than others. Despite my proud days, I really don't want to "fake it till I make it" or be totally independent. I don't want to be Rogue Karen; I want to be Team Karen. I want to do life together with others, each of us contributing where the other falls short so that, as a group, we are strong.

And so does the hearing-impaired person. They, too, want compassion laced with dignity. They carry the heavy responsibility of sorting through muffled words to decipher what the rest of the world is saying. Working hard to hear is exhausting. And, as with my visual struggle, by the end of the day, their hearing seems to be worse because of the exhaustion of working so hard at something so basic.

But it's an inconvenience to walk across the room, look directly in my beloved's face, and articulate without raising my voice or sounding harsh.

It is inconvenient: that's what bearing each other's burdens is all about. We shoulder burdens so we can lighten the load of the one who struggles. Moving closer to a hard-of-hearing person relieves them of the extra steps they must take to hear. When we speak with affection and kindness, we alleviate their anxiety that they are deficient and a burden to the rest of the group. Including them in group conversation reminds them that they belong and they are important.

It is inconvenient: that's what bearing each other's burdens is all about. We shoulder burdens so we can lighten the load of the one who struggles.

Jesus told a story of a shepherd who lost one of his sheep. The shepherd left the flock of ninety-nine other sheep to look for the one lost sheep and bring it back to join the others (see Matt. 18:12–13). I can imagine that, once found, the lost sheep had some special needs. It was probably hungry, dirty, cold, anxious, and maybe even hurt. The shepherd was willing to take time and effort to search for that one sheep, tend to its needs, and bring it home.

No matter what struggles others face—physical disability, mental illness, addiction, or a rough season when life circumstances keep them from being their best—our Lord calls us to go into inclusion mode. We can show compassion laced with dignity and travel the inconvenient extra mile of effort so we can share the load. It might be as simple as moving closer, repeating sentences, offering a ride to the grocery store, waiting extra minutes at the bottom of a wheelchair ramp, or patiently answering questions about faith in Jesus.

Jesus asks us to treat others as we would like to be treated. When we do that for those with special challenges, we diffuse their frustration and empower them to have the courage and energy to keep trying. The words "can't hear you" become less frequent, and they find joy in being included because we've chosen to enter their space and do life with them.

Lord, show me where I need to set aside my own agenda to help someone else who is bearing a heavy load. Show me how I can walk through their struggle with them.

·········· LISTENING WITH OPEN EARS ··········

Who in your life has hearing, sight, physical-movement, learning, or spiritual struggles? God doesn't ask you to take over life for them, but to ease their burden so they can function and accomplish what he's called them to do. How can you help?

20

Fuzzy Sounds

Praise be to the God and Father of our
Lord Jesus Christ, the Father of compassion and
the God of all comfort.
2 CORINTHIANS 1:3

I can't figure out what you are able to see," new acquaintances
have told me.

I understand their confusion. I'm perplexed by my husband's hearing issues all the time. How can he not hear me when I'm standing right in front of him and then overhear another comment when I'm standing in the next room? Or why can't he hear me speak but he can hear the rumble of thunder several miles away?

One day I asked him the question I don't mind others asking me: "What is your world like?"

His answer surprised me. "There's a lack of clarity to the words I hear, an 'almost but not quite' kind of clarity. I can hear part of the words and the inflection, but not everything. I often think, 'If my hearing was a little better, I'd get it.'"

That resonated with me. His "almost but not quite" sounded like my world of blurry blobs. Once I underwent the eye surgery that gave me Better Than Ever vision, objects had more definition and detail. Could hearing be like eyesight, in that diminished hearing blurred actual sound? That noises were more fuzzy than faded?

This led to new questions. What was it like to live as a hearing-impaired person in a sound-distinct world? To be in a crowd where everyone's voices blended into one mushy sound? To try keeping up with a fast-moving, multivoiced conversation while trying to figure out what was said three sentences ago?

Was Jack's reaction to his hearing loss unique, honed to his particular temperament and gender? How did others cope with the inability to hear in a sound-strong world?

I met a clerk in a dollar discount store whose speech bore the telltale signs of someone who'd grown up with a hearing impairment. Some people are reluctant to talk about their physical limitations, but having learned enough about interacting with hearing loss, I wanted to use those skills with others who couldn't hear. I inhaled a breath of courage and asked, "Do you have a hearing issue?"

"Yes," she said, pulling back her hair. "See my hearing aids?"

"Have you been hearing impaired all your life?"

She spent the next five minutes telling me how an oxygen-infused incubator had stripped her hearing when she was born prematurely. She told how customers informed her she shouldn't be working in retail if she couldn't hear.

"Not true," I said. "You can do this. I'm mainly asking so the next time I come into the store, I know to look directly at you."

"Thank you," she said. "Thank you for asking." Her smile showed she meant it.

All of us want to be understood. We long for others to step into our space and share our singular struggles. Most prefer people ask rather than make assumptions. And the questions should go beyond "What's it like?" Inquiries like "What's frustrating to you?" or "How can I best relate with you?" or "What is not helpful?" show that someone is willing to share our lives, make course corrections on their end, and move into our space.

Try it. Listen to the stories of those who are:

- sight or hearing impaired
- homebound for weeks with a broken ankle
- emotionally bound by grief after a death or divorce
- homeless
- from a minority ethnic heritage
- outsiders or newcomers at the same table with old-timers
- single parents
- Christian teenagers attending public schools
- retired and living on a fixed income

What's it like? What's frustrating? What's the best kind of help?

The first step toward compassion is understanding. And the next step is humility—the willingness to admit that our own weakness is an inability to understand the struggles and grief others face.

The final step toward productive compassion is connecting with the One who has helped us—God, the Father of all compassion and comfort. He knows everything about you. He made your human form, so he knows how it operates and sees its capacity for brokenness. Jesus understands what you face because he took on humanness, lived a solitary life during which no one fully understood him, and suffered the worst excruciating pain. He's been there; he gets it. And he is the only one who has the full power, authority, and willingness to do something about it.

All of us want to be understood. We long for others to step into our space and share our singular struggles.

I've experienced God lifting me out of my own pit. My newly acquired understanding empowers me to offer informed compassion to others who suffer and struggle. I may not show compassion perfectly.

I may forget that my beloved is several decibels short of hearing my words, and I may struggle through my own set of weaknesses and bad days to be all that another human needs me to be. The least I can do is point to Jesus and say, "He can help. He loves you, and he'll walk with you. With his strength, you can make it through."

Lord, give me wisdom to understand the weaknesses and struggles those around me face so I can offer them the comfort and compassion you have freely given to me.

LISTENING WITH OPEN EARS

Select someone you can ask about their life and how they cope. Pray that God opens the door for you to have that conversation of understanding and ask him to guide your words and tone so you can convey his brand of compassion.

21

Ear Rings

*By this everyone will know that you are my
disciples, if you love one another.*
JOHN 13:35

"What is it like to have tinnitus?"

We sat at the supper table, enjoying a special treat of pot roast. My question was another attempt to understand my husband's hearing condition. His answer came quickly, as if he were waiting for someone to ask.

"It's a high-pitched ringing that overlays everything," he said.

My hand hesitated over my plate. "Does the ringing keep you from hearing certain things?"

Jack nodded. "It cancels out nature sounds, voices, and other high-pitched noises." He paused. "It's different than not hearing clearly. It's like a barrier that other sounds must penetrate before I can hear them."

Until that moment, I had not understood his struggle with tinnitus. I couldn't figure out what he could and couldn't hear. Some days he had no trouble hearing me; other days, he couldn't hear me no matter what I did. Now I got it. The high-pitched whine in his head blocked whatever he was attempting to hear. Instead of expecting him to hear me, the best way to communicate on those extra difficult days might be nothing more than a hug.

I've felt a similar confusion when sharing the gospel with unbelieving friends. I talk about Jesus, but they don't get it. They come back with arguments about the validity of the Bible, the insanity of sin, the impossibility of only one way to heaven, or the incredulity of a six-day creation. Explaining that "the Bible says . . ." has no meaning for them; why should they accept what that book says? They seem closed to anything I say. It's like an invisible barrier stretches between them and the message I want to give them.

Barriers to belief can come in many forms. The most entrenched obstruction might be a conflicting worldview someone has lived with from birth, one their parents and earlier generations have always accepted and have passed on to them. The fear that their parents might be hurt if they embrace a different view may freeze their feet from moving forward. *If I accept what the Bible says*, they might wonder, *won't I be suggesting that my parents were wrong and they stand condemned?*

Another barrier breaks my heart. Friends blame God for causing or allowing the horrific life events they've experienced. They might believe in Jesus, but voices and images from the past obscure the full measure of grace and love that Jesus holds out to them. The raw emotion taunts them and causes a rejection of any logical explanation of the gospel message. One's head is numb when their heart still hurts.

We can explain the gospel message till we run out of words and air, but it won't connect if the person in front of us faces an impenetrable barrier. How then do we convince them to follow Jesus? How do we scale the wall?

I like what a missionary friend once told me about the group of people he was trying to reach. "You have to do one hundred acts of kindness—and those need to come from a variety of people, not only you—before they'll begin to engage in discussions about biblical doctrine." His words make sense. Nothing speaks as loudly as character, kindness, and good works. The resistant person can disagree with your belief system, but they can't argue with how it has changed you into a kind and moral person, one who is able to endure whatever circumstances you might face. What they see will help them hear.

Modeling God's grace takes time and effort. It means getting close enough to the skeptic to let them see how you live your life. One kind act isn't enough; it's many acts done over and over again. It means staying consistent, being kind wherever you go to whomever you meet. And living a life that dovetails with your words is not just beneficial to unbelievers, because other Christians also need the reminder that God's love is real. Those teetering on the edge of faith need the validation that this Jesus lifestyle really does work and they can do it too.

> Modeling God's grace takes time and effort. It means getting close enough to the skeptic to let them see how you live your life.

It's far easier to preach a sermon or write a blog post. We'd love to win someone over with our compelling words and then move on to the next person. But, as with my husband's tinnitus, barriers can resist the best of presentations. While it might seem the long way around to salvation, grace tells us to soften our approach and win others with kindness—the same kindness God has shown to us.

It's a beautiful day when these barriers show signs of crumbling. In the meantime, don't give up and don't give in to frustration like I often have with Jack's tinnitus. Instead, on those days when people close to you may be particularly pesky about your faith, reach out with something comparable to a hug and wait for another day.

Lord, give me insight into the unbelievers in my life
so I can understand what prevents them from knowing
and accepting you. Nudge me to do those acts of

*kindness that will best penetrate their defenses so
they will consider Christ.*

·········· LISTENING WITH OPEN EARS ··········

Who in your life shows resistance to your faith in Christ? What keeps them from accepting Jesus? If you don't know, spend more time with them, and ask God to show you through conversations what barriers stand between them and full acceptance of God's unfailing love for them.

PART THREE

SOUND INFORMATION
Why We Hear

22
Doorbells

Here I am! I stand at the door and knock. If anyone
hears my voice and opens the door, I will come in
and eat with that person, and they with me.
REVELATION 3:20

*I*n my childhood home, visitors fell into two categories: the back
door group and the front door group. If the front doorbell rang, it
was a pesky salesman, a neighborhood child who lost his ball over our
fence, or a religious peddler. Mom could deal with that, so I'd keep my
nose in my book. But if a knock sounded at the back door, that meant
family, and I'd emerge from my room to see who it was. Grandma and
Grandpa. Our fun single aunt. My brother, home on military leave.

Throughout the years, a knock, doorbell buzz, telephone ring, or
electronic device chime has raised my head from whatever I'm doing.
To me, they represent connection, and these sounds make me smile.
Phone calls from home were welcome breaks in college. When I had
a family of my own, hearing the car pull into the garage after a long,
weary day made me stand straighter and brush a hand through my
hair: my beloved would soon walk through the door.

God created us as social beings. At some point, even the most introverted among us crave human companionship. God designed us, as

beings made in his image, to relate with him. He longs to walk with us, share a meal, and give us his undivided attention. He hopes we feel the same.

But things happen to fracture the joy of relationship. Let's admit it. We have moments when we're not happy to encounter the person on the other side of the door, phone line, or virtual space, even if they stand at the family entrance. One set of grandparents perpetually arrived hours early before holiday dinners, wondering why we kept busy with food preparations rather than sitting down to talk with them. (We weren't ready!) Other life situations, like unresolved conflict, can steal the joy of connection. My reaction to the knock indicates the health and strength of my relationship with the one who's come to visit.

After Adam and Eve ate the forbidden fruit, their now-fractured relationship with God caused them to hesitate at the sound of God's approach in the garden of Eden. A walk with God was no longer a joyful reunion. They had disobeyed him and could no longer meet with him without a flush of shame (see Gen. 3:6–13).

God designed us, as beings made in his image, to relate with him.

The Bible tells of other reactions to God's approach. Mary Magdalene, so excited to see the risen Lord, clung to him (John 20:17). Others weren't so exuberant. Isaiah, seeing the sight and sound of God's holiness, responded with, "I am ruined! For I am a man of unclean lips" (Isa. 6:5). Simon Peter, upon seeing Jesus's power and authority for the first time, implored, "Go away from me, Lord; I am a sinful man!" (Luke 5:8). The people of Israel were terrified at God's voice (Exod. 20:18–19), and their descendants would not listen to God (2 Kings 17:40).

We're no different. We have mixed reactions when God comes near.

Perhaps, like Adam and Eve, we know we've let God down and we're ashamed to look him in the face. Or, not having full access to his plans and purposes, we assume he hasn't kept his promises and we no longer trust all he says. Like the Old Testament Israelites or the ambivalent believers within the church at Laodicea (Rev. 3:14–20), we often allow the things of this earthly life to mute the sound of his presence. We forget to listen for his knock and show excitement that he has come to visit.

If I heard the Lord coming up the walk to my house, how would I respond? I'd like to give the Sunday school answer that I'd throw open the door and shriek, "Jesus!" I'd like to say I'd set my book aside and invite him into the kitchen to make supper with me. We'd linger long past the time the food grew cold as we talked and shared and laughed and reached a new level of intimacy. I wish I could say I'm always ready to receive him and never bothered if he happens to come earlier than I expected or in a way I don't anticipate.

I have a long way to go. I imagine you do too. I want to ask both of us, Why? What's keeping us from actively listening for Jesus's approach? I wonder if beneath the veneer of ambivalence or distraction lies the core of shame. Do we, like our ancestors Adam and Eve, feel unworthy to stand in God's presence? It helps to remember that once we've accepted Jesus's offer of salvation through his death on the cross, "there is now no condemnation for those who are in Christ Jesus" (Rom. 8:1). We have access to his throne room, where he invites us to stride forward in confidence (Heb. 4:16).

God's mercy and grace wait for us. He wants us with him. He accepts us as we are because of who he is and what he has done—not because of what we have done or failed to do. The sound of his knock can bring us streaming out of our corners with awestruck delight, because he has claimed us as family and wants desperately for us to be with him.

Forgive me, Lord, for the times I've ignored your knock.
Today, I let you in. I welcome you to spend the day with me
and join me in whatever I do.

·········· LISTENING WITH OPEN EARS ··········

Record several ways you can include God in your daily routine today.

23

Directions

Whether you turn to the right or to the left, your ears will hear a voice behind you, saying, "This is the way; walk in it."

ISAIAH 30:21

A common way to guide a sight-impaired person is to let them hold your arm above the elbow and then walk in front of them. The person will feel your steps through your motions.

Even with Better Than Ever eyesight, I struggle to see at night or in crowded situations. But since I do have some usable vision, I chafe at the label of "blind" that holding an elbow implies. So when we leave a store and head for the car in a large, dark parking lot, Jack gives me the dignity of normalcy by letting me walk several paces ahead of him. From behind, he quietly gives me verbal directions. "The car is four down on the right. Turn left. Watch out for the speed bump. Stop— car coming."

To the uninformed, Jack may come off as an arrogant, egotistical man who thinks his wife is incapable of remembering where we parked the car or how to dodge a pothole. *Bet he doesn't let her drive either.* They got that right! Driving is not a smart idea for me since I've never had a license and don't know the gas pedal from the brake.

They would be so wrong about his motive, though. Jack is actually allowing me the freedom to walk on my own while giving me the verbal cues I need. If I run into trouble or become disoriented, I can backtrack two paces to hold his hand and look like I'm madly in love with him.

We often interpret the imperative statements in the Bible as commands. We have even labeled one group of directives as the Ten Commandments. We chafe at what we see as rules, rules, and more rules. And in our resistance, we've sometimes painted God to be an arrogant, egotistical taskmaster who tries to control us and tell us what to do.

Maybe not.

Think of God as one who desperately wants us to have the wonderful life he has planned for us (see 1 Cor. 2:9). He's not going to yank us forward, chiding us when we stumble. Instead, he stands with us, his voice speaking through the sound of his written Word, which gives us clear, distinct directions. *Go here. Do this. Stop. Don't go there.* All these commands instruct us on how to arrive at God's best for us and to avoid stumbling into dangers he doesn't intend for us.

Yes, we could do our own thing. We could attempt an alternate route. But God knows there's only one way to get to the destination of an everlasting relationship with him and all other routes lead to dead ends. So doesn't it make sense that he would give us distinct, no-wiggle-room directives? And if we want to reach the eternal paradise heaven offers, wouldn't it be wise on our part to follow what he says?

> All these commands instruct us on how to arrive at God's best for us and to avoid stumbling into dangers he doesn't intend for us.

In the Bible, God often attaches reassurances, reasons, and results to his commands (italics mine):

So do not fear, *for I am with you*; do not be dismayed, *for I am your God. I will strengthen you and help you; I will uphold you with my righteous right hand.* (Isa. 41:10)

Now go; *I will help you speak and will teach you what to say.* (Exod. 4:12)

Keep your lives free from the love of money and be content with what you have, because God has said, *"Never will I leave you; never will I forsake you."* (Heb. 13:5)

Obeying God's directives frees our minds and our energy to focus on the projects and pleasures he has planned for us. It's an alternating relationship. For example, God gives me a command such as loving him more than I love wealth. I obey because I'm willing to trust his better judgment and his ability to take care of me, even when finances are slim. As I put my financial needs in his hands, my mind is then free to concentrate on the big-picture things of earthly life—things that will last into eternity, like strengthening my family and church relationships, and allocating resources toward building up God's kingdom. As I do, God continues to guide and provide, showing me his capability to both meet my personal needs and bring about great results through my devoted efforts on his behalf. He'll show me riches far beyond the wealth of this world that I never could've considered if my mind had been frozen on earthly wealth alone.

Oh, my friend, God loves you so much. He won't give you directions that send you into a pothole. He wants you to safely arrive into a perfectly intimate relationship with him. He has done everything on his end to help you make it into his presence. He's written it out in clear language through the Bible how the two of you can connect. He sent his Son, Jesus, to pay the punishment you deserved for the times you refused to follow his instructions. And he's sent the Holy Spirit to live within you to provide the everyday guidance you need to keep walking forward.

The Lord stands behind you, giving you those directions that will lead you into the most awesome relationship you've ever known. Listen to what he says—that's what will get you home.

> *Lord, thank you for the clear directions you've given me for how to navigate life. Like the best of coaches, you stay nearby to guide me, because you want me to reach the finish line of faith and spend forever with you. Thank you.*

···················· LISTENING WITH OPEN EARS ····················

Choose a Bible verse that tells of a behavior or attitude God wants you to have. Pray that God will show you how to apply that verse throughout your day today.

24
Airplanes

*Now faith is confidence in what we hope for and
assurance about what we do not see.*
HEBREWS 11:1

I was seventeen the first time I boarded a commercial jet, and I
was nervous. I felt like I had stepped onto an alien planet. To make
things worse, instead of sitting with other girls in my 4-H group on
our trip to Washington, DC, my seating assignment was next to a
slouching fifteen-year-old boy who, with one glance, made it clear he
had no use for girls. Trying to be friendly and alleviate my tension, I
commented I was nervous because I'd never flown on a jet before.

It was the right thing to say.

That kid perked up and made it his personal responsibility to explain everything about our flight in terms I could understand. Best of
all, he told me what I would feel and hear, and what it signified.

"When we start down the runway, you'll hear the engines acceler-
ate. You'll feel your body pushed back in the seat and see the front of
the cabin rise as the nose of the plane goes up," he told me. "You'll hear
a change in sound when we lift from the ground, and you'll hear the
landing gear and wing flaps retract."

He remained quiet throughout the bulk of the trip. Then, forty-five minutes before landing, he perked up again. "Listen for the change of sound in the engines," he said. When I showed delight that I could hear it, he added, "It always happens. That's your cue that we are beginning our descent." He went on to describe new sounds: the raising of the flaps, the lowering of the landing gear, and the final thrust of the engine before the wheels touched the pavement.

I was enthralled. My seatmate's information about the workings of an airplane gave me reassurance we would reach our destination and helped me jettison my fears of the unknown. I now love to fly, and on every flight since that initial trip, I've found pleasure in listening for the changing sound that indicates we are starting our descent.

Flight is an act of faith for any passenger. Despite my accrued knowledge, I'm still relying on the skill of engineers, pilots, and air traffic controllers to get me where I'm going. Confidence in their years of experience is crucial if I don't care to have a mental meltdown midflight. And since I'm not on the flight deck with the pilot, seeing the final approach, I take on faith that the sounds of descent still mean what they have indicated in past flights.

Stepping into a life of faith in Christ can seem like we've entered an alien culture. Uncertainty over what it might entail can be unnerving. But trust in Jesus is not a blind faith. It is based on evidence found in the Bible and our own growing experience with the ways of God that validate the reliability of what we've read.

Trust in Jesus is not a blind faith.

We also have the testimony of countless Christ followers who have gone before us. Hebrews 11 gives a passenger list of people who dared to believe and emerged on the other side of doubts and struggles, their faith stronger than before. So many people that the writer of Hebrews admits he doesn't have time to mention them all (v. 32).

During their earthly lifetime, many of those listed in Hebrews 11 didn't get to see God fulfill his promise to send Jesus the Messiah.

They faced perilous journeys that were anything but textbook flights. But they held on to their faith because they had confidence in what they hoped for—the coming of the Anointed One, who would reset all things back to their intended place and purpose (Heb. 11:39–40).

How can you grow more confident about your faith in Jesus? The more you know about God—his character, works, plans, and purpose—the more conviction you'll have that following Jesus is worth the journey. You'll meet people who have run the race or flown the flight before you: informed, experienced people who will tell you what to watch and listen for so you'll know you are headed in the right direction. You'll learn how to recognize danger signs and how to respond if you do encounter threats. You'll learn more of what Jesus has done to overcome evil and its demonic representative so you can say with confidence, "Greater is He who is in [me] than he who is in the world" (1 John 4:4 NASB).

As you learn more about God, the knowledge you gain will tell you faith in Christ is trustworthy, and the experience you acquire by taking active steps of faith will assure you that it does work.

In a commercial jet, a wall separates us from the pilot who sits at the control panel and the front window showing our destination's runway. But the sounds of the airplane tell us we're almost there. Likewise, trapped in this earthly world, we can't visibly see the final path to the terminal of heaven. But God's constant presence, his words in the Bible, and the witness we hear and see from other believers give us the confidence we need to keep moving forward. They encourage us that we're almost home.

*Thank you, Lord, for giving me indicators throughout my
life that assure me I'm on the right path toward you.*

········· **LISTENING WITH OPEN EARS** ·········

Who, through their life of faith, has given you evidence that faith in Christ is worth the risk? Find a way to thank that person for being a model of faith for you.

25

Sirens

*May the God of hope fill you with all joy and peace
as you trust in him, so that you may overflow with
hope by the power of the Holy Spirit.*
ROMANS 15:13

*O*ur community in Kansas was so small that if we heard an emergency vehicle's siren, the odds were five to one we knew the people involved. We would exhale a quiet "oh no" and think the worst: car accident, prairie fire, house fire, injury, or death for one of our friends or acquaintances. We'd rattle off a list of precious church members who lived on the edge of debilitating health crises. We'd bow our heads, praying for those involved, and wait by the telephone for the inevitable call from someone who would tell us who, what, and how. Later, we'd tell the people involved and the emergency personnel that we had prayed, and their eyes would brim with tears. "Thank you. You have no idea how much we needed that."

Years later, in another state, I changed my reaction to sirens. This time I was on the other side of that distant wail. Heading home from a graduation, I tripped on uneven pavement in a hotel parking lot, twisted my ankle, and fell forehead-first onto broken asphalt. A distraught Jack disappeared to get help from the front desk clerk, who quickly determined a cloth was not enough to stop the steady stream of blood spilling onto the pavement. EMTs responded quickly and the sound of approaching sirens filled me with hope and relief; those sirens were coming for me. Their piercing melody sang me a reassuring song: *Help is on the way.*

Now, as a resident in a large city in yet another state, where EMTs and victims are strangers, sirens bring even more comfort. I felt their song of hope one night when police helicopters kept vigilance over our neighborhood and police cars voiced their presence on a nearby main thoroughfare. They were looking for an armed and dangerous thief who'd robbed a pharmacy, stolen a vehicle, and been spotted heading into the neighborhood west of us. The drone and whine of copter and car told me, *We're here. We're watching out for you. We're on this.* Hope ruled my heart that, for us, the story would end well—and it did.

Hope speaks sound into the silence and tells us *help is on the way.* I don't even want to think about the consequences if I had been by myself when I fell and there had been no sirens coming to give medical assistance. In that case, the silence would have been serious and could have been deadly.

When we put our faith in Christ, the hope connected with our faith draws us into a higher dimension. Hope claims we are not on a dead-end street; instead, it offers a purpose and promises a destination. All of God's work in our lives tells us, as I discovered after my miraculous eye surgery, that there's more to the story than our current life circumstances. Our story's ending *will* be Better Than Ever. Even if the sounds of earth hold no assurance of rescue, we grasp on to the hope that God is bigger than anything we face. Help is not just on the way; it is already beside us.

That's the beauty behind Paul's benediction given in Romans 15:13. When we trust God to care for us and for others, we get the payoff of peace and joy because we know everything is under God's control. The combination of joy, peace, and trust culminates in a bumper crop of hope. Confidence that there's more to the story. Assurance that this isn't the end. A rock-solid certainty that there is someone powerful enough to restrain the out-of-control spin our bodies and brains want to convince us we've entered.

God is bigger than anything we face.

Jack and I still pray for the person on the other side of the sirens we hear, because we've come to realize that prayer is a powerful tool of hope. Our prayers for those in trouble bring God into the equation of the crisis and invite him to be part of the solution. I've learned to pray that God will make his presence known to the person who's in trouble—that they may see God in action. I pray that they find confidence that God will get them through whatever they face.

What sounds alert you to ask God to impart hope to the hurting? Whether for stranger or friend, you can pray that the one in crisis will reach out to God and discover the beautiful joy and peace that come when we trust him. You may not receive an in-person thank-you for your prayers, and you will likely never hear the resolution to the story behind the sirens. Regardless, you will have deep-down satisfaction that you have partnered with God to bring healing and hope to a stranger.

And if you are ever the one at the destination of an inbound siren, you can thank God for those within earshot who are quietly lifting your unknown name to the Father. Thank the Lord that joy and peace can be found through trusting in him. Through the hope God has given you, you have the assurance that he is with you and you are not alone.

Lord, thank you for the gift of hope that reminds me you are in charge and you have more to write in my story.

LISTENING WITH OPEN EARS

The next time you hear a siren, stop what you are doing and ask God to make his presence known to the people involved, that they will find peace in knowing that God sees their need and is there to help.

26

Footsteps

Since we live by the Spirit,
let us keep in step with the Spirit.
GALATIANS 5:25

*C*reating a replica of a sound is not as simple as you might think. Early producers of radio theater discovered this when they began adding what are known as Foley sound effects to story narratives so listeners would have a better idea of the action taking place. Producers had to recreate the exact sounds of specific noises, taking into account that each sound carried a suitcase full of story variables: who and what was making the sound, the location and force of the sound, and so much more.

Take, for example, a footstep. A lady's high heels on a tile floor in a high-ceilinged room will sound different than a child's running steps on a playground or a man's heavy work boots climbing stairs. Most of us would have trouble identifying an isolated noise on a soundtrack, but attached to a storyline, we sure would know if the radio theater producers didn't get the right match. Something would seem off.

We put ID tags on sounds all the time. We can identify a person merely by listening to their footsteps, and we can determine whether those footsteps are within the realm of normal or whether we should be concerned. If I hear the back door open and close shortly after noon and then a heavy footfall that sounds like a size twelve loafer, I know my husband has come home for lunch. But if I heard the back door close and the sound of a quiet athletic shoe at two in the morning, I would have cause for concern. The sound wouldn't fit my concept of "normal."

Deducing facts about a person by listening only to their footsteps reaches the pay grade of a forensics detective or a Foley artist. Discerning the difference between good and evil can be just as daunting. The Tree of the Knowledge of Good and Evil in the garden of Eden makes the dilemma sound easy. Good and evil, black and white. Right? But in the eons of time since Adam and Eve became acquainted with the difference, the infiltration of evil in the world has blurred the lines. Some days, it's hard to know whether something is good or evil. I have days when I stand between two conflicting voices, looking from one to the other and thinking, "I don't know who to believe!" And the devil can be sly in making evil look good and good look despicable.

How are we supposed to know?

It took years of practice and routine for me to recognize Jack's footsteps. We've been married long enough now that I can pick his footfall out in a crowd of people. In the same way, I can go to God, the source of all good, and learn what good looks like. "Every good and perfect gift is from above, coming down from the Father of the heavenly lights," says James 1:17. God is the source of all goodness and righteousness (Ps. 145:7). It may take years of observing God's character and actions to identify good and evil, and we may still be perplexed about whether a particular choice is good or whether a certain belief system is from God. But if God is the originator of what is good and we know the Father well enough—his patterns, track record, and predictable ways of acting—we will sense the better choice.

It's not always easy. Satan is the master of lies and subtle deception. He can appear as an angel of light. If he used Scripture quotes to tempt Jesus in the wilderness (see Matt. 4:6), he'll play with your mind too. He'll make you wonder about your motives. He'll fill your mind with the benefits of a choice without including the drawbacks or long-term consequences. You'll hear in your mind, *A little won't hurt*, or *You have to take care of yourself.* And then there's his standby, the classic argument he used with Eve that first time in Eden: *Did God really say you couldn't do that?* (see Gen. 3:1). And it will all sound so plausible, so . . . *good.*

> If God is the originator of what is good and we know the Father well enough—his patterns, track record, and predictable ways of acting—we will sense the better choice.

We can overrule the taunts and twisted truths we hear from the Evil One. We can learn to sniff out evil and sense when something doesn't fit into God's normal pattern of doing things. When we hear a news report about a world event, listen to encouragement to embrace a certain lifestyle choice, or face soft lies and harsh criticism from others about our own choices, we can, with God's help, figure out how we should live. Like the sound of high heels tapping a tile floor to represent a child running across a soccer field, we'll be able to discern when something isn't quite right. In those moments, we can run to our heavenly Father in prayer and beg, "Help me know the truth."

How can you better recognize the difference between good and evil?

1. Get to know God very well.
Learn to recognize his footsteps, which never change or deceive.

2. As you come to know him better, listen carefully to each situation.
Dig beneath the surface and observe the details of what you see and hear. Be ever aware that Satan is out to trip you up—he has his own agenda, and it is never good.

3. Follow him more closely by getting into habits of righteousness.

Look at choices not only in terms of good or bad, but good, better, and best. Choose the best and don't settle for less. In most contexts, some things are permissible but not always beneficial or constructive, as Paul warns in 1 Corinthians 10:23. Don't negotiate or rationalize. You wouldn't minimize those stealthy footsteps at two in the morning; why rationalize the warning sounds of worldly choices?

Above all, stay in step with the Spirit who lives within you. That's an everyday commitment as we learn to say each morning, "Lord, I choose you. This day, I will follow you." Stay close to the Lord throughout your day and his footsteps will lead you where you need to go.

Father, I want to become so familiar with your ways that I can better recognize the difference between good and evil and choose what you see as good. Help me.

·········· LISTENING WITH OPEN EARS ··········

In what area do you have trouble distinguishing between good and evil? Spend time analyzing the situation. Ask yourself: *How would God be honored? How would Satan be honored?* Ask God for wisdom and discernment to know the best choice.

27

Teakettles

Today, if you hear his voice, do not harden
your hearts.

HEBREWS 4:7

*W*arning: I'm lethal with teakettles.

My first was a simple ivory ceramic-clad kettle, filled with orange petaled flowers—the centerpiece at my wedding shower. With my love of hot tea, a close friend knew it was the perfect gift for me. I loved that teakettle. It became much loved and much used.

Over time, I would fill my kettle, turn on the stove, and then move toward other things. I'd hear the change in sound announcing my water was near the boiling point, but I'd ignore it. It would be there waiting for me.

Jack tried to be helpful. "Karen! Your water's boiling."

"Oh. Ok."

Pause, pause, pause.

"Karen."

"I know!"

It took me two years to kill it.

Sent home early from work one day due to sickness, I put the kettle on for a cup of tea and lay down while waiting for the water to boil. An hour later, the smell of scorched metal woke me.

I don't remember the second kettle. I only remember that I ruined that one too. I'd become very adept at putting the kettle on and then ignoring the sound of boiling water. Jack decided to save money on teakettle replacement, not to mention potential kitchen fires, and bought me a whistling teakettle.

I found a way to ignore the whistle.

During a particularly brutal Midwest winter, we wanted steam in the house, so we circumvented the whistle by sticking the handle end of a spoon in the spout. Jack went off to work and I, well . . .

Enter teakettle number four.

Bless the day my unsuspecting nephew gave us an electric kettle with a thirty-minute shutoff feature.

I don't want to ignore the voice of God like I ignore teakettles. The effects of disregarding God's voice may not be felt in thirty minutes, but they are certainly more disastrous. We're not talking about only a kettle or a house. A flagrant, unyielding resistance to God can set into motion a string of consequences that will cause irrevocable damage to our earthly lives, the lives of others, and God's kingdom.

> A flagrant, unyielding resistance to God can set into motion a string of consequences that will cause irrevocable damage to our earthly lives, the lives of others, and God's kingdom.

Yet, at times, I feel that hardness creep into my life. The Spirit of God reminds me to show patience and speak with love, and I feel my jaw clench while an inner voice whispers back, *I don't wanna be nice.* Or as I begin the path of my morning prayer and Bible study, my mind meanders toward other activities—the coffeepot, a game on my electronic device, a few more moments of sleep—and I stray from the things that keep my spirit soft and flexible. And then there are those days where ambivalence reigns and I counter God's persistent voice with, *It can wait.*

God's voice reverberates throughout my day. He speaks through the words of his Word. His Spirit might echo something I read that morning or bring to mind a principle I've known for years. He combines his written directives with specific applications, nudging me toward the right time and the specific people who need me to bring his grace and mercy. For example, he might press a name and need of a lonely friend into my mind and stir my reluctance with a reminder from Galatians 6:9: "Let us not become weary in doing good." But all of this accomplishes nothing if I turn away and don't respond.

Many have written on how to know God's will for our lives. Yet perhaps we need to spend equal time learning how to move forward once we do hear God's voice, when we do know for certain what his will is.

The Bible tells of people who actively chose to ignore and disobey. God commanded the Israelite nation to leave Egypt and trust his leading to a land of freedom and prosperity. Well, it wasn't long before the people complained about God's decision to bring them into a desert wasteland with no water (Exod. 17:1–7). Their resistance was so noteworthy that the psalmist mentions it in Psalm 95 and the writer of Hebrews includes it in a warning: "Today, if you hear his voice, do not harden your hearts as you did in the rebellion, during the time of testing in the wilderness" (Heb. 3:7–8).

The Bible addresses our tendency to drag our feet as well. When two men were presented with the option to follow Jesus, one said he wanted to bury his father first and the other asked to say goodbye to his family. Jesus's reply? "No one who puts his hand to the plow and looks back is fit for service in the kingdom of God" (Luke 9:62). Jesus's message? Don't delay. Do it now.

Today, if you hear his voice, do not harden your hearts.

Do you have trouble hearing God's voice? Are you feeling like you don't know what he wants you to do? Start with what you know.

Write down his directives. And as you read, ask, *God, how can I apply this—today?* When the Spirit shows you how to connect the Word with your life, do it. Don't harden your heart. Don't think it will wait for later.

Let the sound of his voice and the imprint of his Word spur you to action—today.

> *Lord, I want to do a better job of listening and responding to your voice. Show me the hard spots in my heart where I have resisted what you have told me to do.*

LISTENING WITH OPEN EARS

Write down three ways to obey God that you have learned from Scripture. Pray that God will show you how to do those things today. Ask him to remind you in the moment to obey what he has asked.

28

Tornado Warnings

*Whoever dwells in the shelter of the Most High will
rest in the shadow of the Almighty.*
PSALM 91:1

One peek out my kitchen window told me the tornado siren was not malfunctioning. The sky was as dark as twilight. Tree limbs bent and swayed as if ushering me toward the basement's safety. I scooped up my friend's poodle that we were watching while she vacationed, and called for Jack and our daughter to get downstairs. Punctuating the urgency, a crack of lightning turned off our electricity.

Jack made it halfway down the narrow steps and then turned back. The wind howled louder. "What are you doing?" I hissed.

"Getting a flashlight," he said.

He was gone longer than it should have taken to find his stash. I wasn't in a mood to be diplomatic. "What took you so long?"

"I peeked my head out the door to look at the storm."

And he scolds me for ignoring teakettles? My heart moved to my throat. *Don't do this to me.*

We stayed huddled in the basement for nearly forty-five minutes while a vicious thunderstorm raged above us. When the all-clear signal replaced the noise of the wind, we headed upstairs and checked our house and property for damage—none! Then, as folks do in rural small towns, we headed for the car to see if neighbors needed help. We first went to our friend's house. The weather forecast had said nothing about twisters, but the disarray on her deck looked as if a giant hand had rotated her furniture by a quarter turn.

All of us—even Jack—were very glad we'd heeded that warning call.

Humans have learned that we can use sound as a warning system for impending danger. One person can broadcast what they see and know to multitudes who cannot yet see or know. I'm deeply thankful that modern technology can predict and broadcast bad weather. Jack and I could tell countless stories of entire neighborhoods that were saved because someone sounded the alarm. I imagine you can too.

It's as old a practice as the night watchmen of biblical times (Ezek. 33:2), the town crier of the medieval era, and the air raid sirens during the London Blitz of World War II. It happens on the spiritual level too: Jonah walked through Nineveh, calling out the consequences if the people didn't repent (Jonah 3:1–5).

It's tragic when groups of people don't listen to warnings. The Bible carries plenty of those stories. Noah preached righteousness to his generation but only eight people rode the waves of the great flood to safety (2 Peter 2:5). Both Moses and Jeremiah reminded their audiences multiple times of God's warnings, of the terrible things that would happen if they didn't stay true to his commands, but the people wouldn't listen. The hard lesson is this: the systems intended to save lives won't work if people don't take action. The consequences are as real in the spiritual realm as they are during severe thunderstorms.

Why don't people—then or now—obey the sounds of warning when the danger is so clear? Based on the times I haven't zipped down the steps to my basement, I can speculate on why human nature tends to disregard warnings. In the case of weather systems, we don't want to believe the danger is as immanent or potentially damaging as the sirens make it sound. *I'm here, I know what it's like outside, it's not that bad*, we reason. We want to believe there's no danger, no consequences, and no hurry.

That might work with weather predictions. As we all know, forecasters are as fallible as any human. But it doesn't work so well with God's warnings and commands. For when we think *it's not that bad*, or *one little dabble won't hurt me*, we are acting as if we know our situation better than God does. In doing so, we push God away and set ourselves up to be in charge.

The systems intended to save lives won't work if people don't take action. The consequences are as real in the spiritual realm as they are during severe thunderstorms.

Psalm 91 is a beautiful song of God's watchful care for those who trust in him. The words assure us we have no need to fear the scary stuff, for God will be a shield and refuge for us. But there's a catch. His protection is available to those who seek him. "Whoever *dwells* in the shelter of the Most High will rest in the shadow of the Almighty" (v. 1, italics added). If we want God's protection, we need to position ourselves behind his safety net. I have a far better chance of surviving a devastating tornado if I dwell in my basement during the storm. But it's my choice to get down into the basement.

I show my trust in God by following his directions, even when it doesn't seem like the danger is too great. The damage from past poor choices reminds me that God truly does have the better idea of how to live. His warning systems, in fact, prove the extent of his love for me. He didn't merely give one-time commands and then leave us to suffer the consequences of disobedience. He loves us enough to give warnings, and he spells out what will happen if we don't listen.

He goes a step further. He assures us of the blessing and security we'll experience if we heed his voice. He provides a shield that protects and sustains us when everything is falling apart around us.

I'm so grateful for the shelter of his love.

> *Lord, forgive the times I have disregarded your commands and chosen my own way. Thank you for the shelter and security you offer when we decide to follow and obey you.*

LISTENING WITH OPEN EARS

Where is your safe spot during a severe storm? How is your safe spot like God's spiritual protection over your life? How do God's commands protect you from danger?

29

Implosions

I have told you these things, so that in me you may
have peace. In this world you will have trouble. But
take heart! I have overcome the world.
JOHN 16:33

I used to think controlled building implosions were exciting. I'd watch video after video of high-rise structures belting out puffs of smoke like one hundred lit cigars and then folding in on themselves. So precise. Such well thought-out planning with minimal damage to surrounding buildings. The engineering feat fascinated me.

When I heard about the scheduled demolition of a high-rise dormitory at a nearby university, I begged Jack to take us and talked excitedly to friends in our small town about it. But some didn't share my enthusiasm. "That's the dorm I stayed in when I attended college," several told me. Emotional attachment and personal history marred their curiosity about the demolition process.

Undaunted, Jack and I staked out space on a nearby hill to watch the proceedings. What had once been fascinating head knowledge based on impersonal videos now became real. I heard the rumbles, smelled the smoke, and saw the building crumble into a self-made crater. The precision explosions of dynamite popped louder than gunfire.

A rumble more menacing than thunder shook the ground beneath our feet. Billows of smoke blazed a trail across the clear blue sky.

I'm glad I wasn't any closer than I was. I would have seen and heard steel columns twist into molten metal and rock-solid cement crumble into dust. I don't even want to think about standing at the window of a building next door or, more horrifying, being inside the imploding structure.

Implosion is the sudden, violent inward collapse of a building. The explosives knock out the building's inner vertical supports, causing upper floors to pancake from the weight above which puts added pressure on the rest of the building so it smashes down on itself. The process won't happen if the core structure isn't initially weakened by the explosives.

Maybe your mind is going where mine is. I think about current social structures that have weakened through corruption, mismanagement, greed, and selfish motives. How can a society stay strong when the smaller parts are splintering in so many directions? We watch the breakup of the family unit and the corrosion of the very definition of family. We grieve over the choices friends make that may compromise their future well-being. And we fear that if enough friends, families, and communities break down, at some point our entire society might buckle, and we might be sucked into the destruction as well.

Biblical and historical records do give examples of societal destruction. In Genesis, God reduced two cities, Sodom and Gomorrah, to smoking rubble for their wicked ways. Other kingdoms, like the Hittite and Roman Empires, are likewise no more. They fell, not necessarily because a stronger world power overcame them but because they had compromised their own strength through a string of self-destructive choices.

Does this stir up a sense of distress within you? Do you fear that as we see segments of our society crumbling, you'll be caught in the implosion? More personally, as you see trouble after trouble threatening to remove what is important to you, like an invisible hand removing Jenga tiles from your life tower, do you envision yourself collapsing into a pile of rubble along with the rest of the world?

Oh, beloved of Jesus, have peace. Your knees may feel weak and wobbly, but Jesus will help you stand strong. It might sound utterly impossible, but remember, Jesus specializes in the impossible. Society may fall; the church will not. Jesus has promised the church will stand as solid as a rock and nothing will prevail against it (see Matt. 16:18). So put your faith in him. You will endure, even overcome, if you depend on the strength of the One who made you, knows you, loves you, and redeems you.

Oh, beloved of Jesus, have peace.
Your knees may feel weak and wobbly,
but Jesus will help you stand strong.
Society may fall; the church will not.

You may have to watch the destruction. You may stand at a distance like Abraham did when Sodom and Gomorrah fell. Or, like the angels who pulled Lot and his family to safety, the Lord may whisk you out of the very edges of the firestorm. Today especially, Christians may be mocked and blamed for society's problems and Christian practices banned outright. But Jesus said, "The one who stands firm to the end will be saved" (Matt. 24:13). Take comfort in this: even if you were to lose all this world has to offer, when you don't relinquish your faith in Christ, no one—nothing—in this world can crush your soul.

Jesus told a story of two houses. One was built on a solid rock foundation and the other on loose sand. When storms came, the house built on bedrock stood fast, but the one on loose sand fell with a great crash. If we structure our life priorities according to Jesus's plan, we will still witness storms—vicious storms that threaten to rip apart everything we know and love. But don't be alarmed, says Jesus (v. 6). The foundation of your faith and the structural integrity of your soul will not be compromised. The faltering of society won't pull you under. The destruction and chaos of this world will not keep you from heaven.

So don't let the weakening world trouble you. Jesus predicted this would happen, and he has already overcome. If you walk daily with Jesus and put your trust in his power and authority, God will keep you safe from whatever happens in this world.

Oh Lord, keep me strong. Enable me to stay faithful to you all the way to the end. No matter what happens in the world, in my country, or within my family, I want to cling to you and gain my strength from you.

LISTENING WITH OPEN EARS

Do you know a Christ follower who lives within the midst of a disintegrating situation: work, family, or school? Pray that today, God will keep them strong.

PART FOUR

SOUND COMMUNICATION
Who Hears Us

30

Ancient Words

The law of the LORD is perfect, refreshing the soul.
The statutes of the LORD are trustworthy, making
wise the simple.

PSALM 19:7

*M*y senior year in college was a tough year. Barely recovered from a bout of bronchitis, I contracted the kind of food poisoning where one moment you are afraid you'll die and the next moment you fear you won't. The college health clinic prescribed an antinauseant that, one day later, sent me home and then to the hospital emergency room with a rare allergic reaction. With my parents' criticism of how I was mismanaging my life ringing in my ears, I returned to college, only to get sick again.

Defeated, I lay on my dorm room bed, wondering if I would ever get well enough to finish my degree program. My roommate knelt beside my bed. "Can I read the Bible to you?" she asked.

At my suggestion, Beth turned to Romans 8 and read the entire chapter. And it felt like we'd both stepped foot into God's throne room. The first words brought healing to my heartsick soul: "Therefore, there is now no condemnation for those who are in Christ Jesus" (v. 1). In that moment, I wondered how words written two thousand years before could speak to the defeat of one college student and relay the peace and courage she needed to move forward in faith and trust.

The power of the divinely spoken Word brought our world into existence when God first uttered, "Let there be light" (Gen. 1:3). Over the next six days, God verbally directed new layers of creation, one for each day, culminating in the best of his design—people. To this highest class alone, God gave the gift of language. He did this so he could talk to us and we could respond to him. Language gave us the means to relate with each other so we could pass forward to the next generation the knowledge and grace of God.

The power of the divinely spoken Word brought our world into existence.

God equipped ancient people with the ability to put oral language into written form so his people could record his love story. Through the pens of the Old and New Testament writers and the power of the Holy Spirit, the words took on a life of their own, reaching across all generations and cultures to speak truth and wisdom. The message was specific enough not to be vague and confusing but broad enough to provide overarching principles to a myriad of life situations in a way that doesn't straitjacket the reader.

Psalm 19, a beautiful mix of prose and poetry, praises God's twofold strategy to communicate with his beloved children through creation and his written Word. "The heavens declare the glory of God; the skies proclaim the work of his hands" (v. 1). Later, the psalmist describes God's decrees and precepts as "more precious than gold, than much pure gold; they are sweeter than honey" (v. 10). Why so precious and sweet? The ancient words of the Bible invite us to converse with the almighty God, to better understand and appreciate who he is and all he has done.

Those ancient words are not dead words. Although initially written centuries ago, they continue to carry meaning and relevancy. God structured the revelation of his Word in just the right way so each generation can pass his story on to the next and we can remind each other of our connection to God. "Consequently, faith comes from hearing the message, and the message is heard through the word about Christ," says Romans 10:17.

Readers across the centuries have unrolled scrolls or opened books to read them aloud, and listeners often stand to hear the reading of God's Word, for they, too, feel a sense of the holy as the written reverts back to the spoken. The written Word of God itself is powerful, but the spoken sound of God's Word stands on a stage of its own. It becomes living and holy, fresh and personal. It moves past all the minutiae of our lives and speaks directly to our inner spirit, convicting us of what is right, convincing us of what is true, and calming the inflamed edges of our travel-torn souls.

Beth's soft voice concluded the reading with those life-restoring words from Romans 8: "In all these things we are more than conquerors through him who loved us" (v. 37). Because I had accepted what Jesus offered me through his death on the cross, nothing—life or death, my present situation, or anything in the future—would separate me from God's love. I relaxed into peace and within twenty-four hours, my weakened body had grabbed on to renewed health.

God's spoken and written words are "alive and active" (Heb. 4:12). He created all the components of sound and language to make them so. That's how much he longed to talk with us, so we could discover him.

Thank you, Lord, for speaking words into our lives that remind us of your presence, power, and love. Thank you for expressing those words in ways we can understand so we can relate with you, the all-powerful God.

···· LISTENING WITH OPEN EARS ····

Read Psalm 19 slowly several times. How does God speak through creation? How does he speak to us through his Word, the Bible?

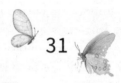

31

Radio Transmissions

We are therefore Christ's ambassadors,
as though God were making his appeal through
us. We implore you on Christ's behalf:
Be reconciled to God.
2 CORINTHIANS 5:20

While our family lived in a rural section of Kansas, a new Christian radio station moved into our area. Our excitement was short-lived—the station was sixty miles away, too far for us to receive the signal. But that excitement was rekindled when we heard the radio station planned to dot the landscape with a series of repeaters. In subsequent years, we smiled every time we heard a station DJ say the name of our area when he read the call letters of each repeater station at the top of the hour. *Yes! We hear you loud and clear.*

Simply put, a repeater transmits a basic radio or television signal at a different frequency that a distant audience can receive. While radio repeaters aren't as prevalent now due to the inception of internet streaming, the concept of extending a message is common in our everyday lives. Cell towers convert signals from one phone and send them on to the destination of the receiving phone. A car transmission moves power from the engine to the wheels.

In the human realm, an ambassador has the same job as a radio re-peater, car transmission, or cell tower. That person carries the message of the country they represent to a foreign group, presenting and trans-lating it with words the audience can understand. The Bible uses this term, *ambassadors*, to describe the role Christians have. God uses us to communicate his Word to those who aren't in direct contact with his words and ways. We proclaim God's message with language, words, and actions that resonate with them at their frequency.

> God uses us to communicate his Word to those who aren't in direct contact with his words and ways.

I remember the first time I was an ambassador for Jesus. One sum-mer week, I worked as a counselor at a Christian youth camp. A ten-year-old boy, a student in the Sunday school class I taught, came to that week of camp. He was having a difficult time, a virtual case study for how kids with challenging home lives act out. He was a constant discipline problem, so much so that older adults rolled their eyes any time his name came up in conversation. All week, I prayed for him. As his teacher, I perceived his inner hurt and loneliness. I so wanted him to meet Jesus the Savior. I knew he understood, at least in his head, who Jesus was and why he'd come to earth; was he ready to make the message his own?

The final evening of camp, I felt an overwhelming urge to talk to Nathan. *No*, I reasoned to myself, *you want him to accept faith in Jesus so much, you think you hear God telling you to go talk to him.* The urge didn't go away. So I prayed: *You know I don't see well, Lord. If this is from you, help me find Nathan in this crowd of kids.* I turned around. There he was, standing by himself.

Shrugging my shoulders at God's tenacity, I asked Nathan if we could talk. "Have you thought about becoming a Christian?" I asked. *That was rather blunt,* I thought.

"Oh, Miss Karen, I can't do that," he said. "I'm too bad."

Lord, I prayed, *help me shape my words in terms he can understand.* I explained how Jesus came to die for bad children and bad adults— how all of us are bad; that's why the Bible calls us sinners. Through faith in him, though, we can take on Jesus's goodness. Nathan and I prayed together that night, and I called his pastor to talk about his baptism. No one could miss the change in Nathan from that moment on.

And me? I wanted to experience the thrill of leading someone to faith in Christ again and again and again.

I've had other chances to spell out the plan of salvation to others. Some have moved forward to take that pivotal step, and many have not. Yet over the years, I've learned that sharing the steps of how to cross the line into faith in Christ is not the only way we transmit the voice of God. In fact, as Christ followers, every word we speak and every action we take have impact for the kingdom of God, whether it helps, hinders, or seemingly does nothing.

We're all working at this together. No one person gets full credit for leading anyone to faith. Notable people have provided those final few words nudging crowds of seekers to cross into Christian faith, but many other unseen believers have added to that moment. No, we don't repeat the plan of salvation four hundred times. Instead, as we'll discover in the next few chapters, we shape our words to the moment, speaking what the hearer is ready to hear, whether it's words of kindness, grace, wisdom, or truth. We become a representative of God in all we say and do. We no longer live for ourselves; instead, we represent Jesus in our words and actions (2 Cor. 5:15).

Each of us contributes to the package of proclamation. We all stand, shoulder to shoulder, in a welcoming line, transmitting the message of God's Word in ways each person will comprehend. Through everything we do and say, the peace, joy, and hope we express communicate the integrity of our faith in God.

*Lord, I accept the role of representing you. Guide whatever
I say throughout my day so my words will bring honor, not
reproach, to your holy name.*

············· LISTENING WITH OPEN EARS ·············

Who will hear your words today? How will the words of your casual
conversations bring honor to Jesus?

32

Words of Grace

Let your conversation be always full of grace,
seasoned with salt, so that you may know how to
answer everyone.
COLOSSIANS 4:6

"*C*ome back."

Tears dripped off the end of my nose and I scrubbed my eyes with a public bathroom paper towel. During a large potluck gathering, I'd sat at a table where the group of women all knew each other and I knew no one. After being openly snubbed twice, I collected my things, rose from the table with a less than gracious rebuke, and fled to the bathroom to consider my options. I wanted to leave. But everyone would see my puffy face if I went back to the meeting room to retrieve my potluck dish.

Two women, realizing what had happened, searched for me in the parking lot. Another checked the bathroom, where she found me in tears.

"I can't come. My face is a mess," I replied to her invitation.

"That's okay." She put a hand on my shoulder. "Sit beside me. We want you with us."

Never were words so sweet. They rivaled the taste of any chocolate on the dessert table. Hearing Dani's words made me grateful that God constructed language to have power to bring comfort and restoration among his children. Dani's grace-filled speech, laced with apologies of her own for the group's behavior, ultimately welcomed me into a circle of precious women with whom I've built enduring friendships.

God has placed all the building blocks of speech at our disposal: the physiology of our mouths, tongues, and vocal cords; the gift of sound; and the myriad combinations of grammar and syntax into meaningful sentences. He asks us to combine these gifts into messages that express his grace and love. Like any other gift from his hand, he requests that we use it to bring him glory: to do good and not harm.

It's the best and easiest gift to pass forward. As God's words impact me, my words will have impact on those who hear me. Whatever noise I allow to come out of my mouth, others will hear. They will react and respond, directly or inwardly. That's the basis of communication.

> God asks us to combine the building blocks of speech into messages that express his grace and love.

But unlike God's words, which reflect his unchanging nature, my words are sometimes infected with the sin disease that infiltrates our world. What I say can act like a warm blanket and cup of tea to the one shaking with fever or fear. But my speech can also be as irritating and harmful as nails scratching across an old-fashioned chalkboard. My choice of words can speak truth that leads to freedom, or it can deceive, sending my listeners to wander aimlessly in confusion. Words can carry barbs of criticism, ripping into another's self-confidence and making them afraid to move forward in life. Or they can offer grace and forgiveness that beckon fellow travelers into the circle of God's love.

We get to choose what we do with God's amazing gift of words. We can bless or curse (James 3:10). We can showcase God's unconditional love or manipulate others to our own self-interests.

That day, in the bathroom, Dani chose words of grace.

God gives us the privilege of language so we can impart his grace to those around us. Yet, as James tells his readers, grace-laced words cannot be an erratic occurrence, giving praise to one and pain to another (James 3:9–12). If we want to bless others, then gracious and appealing words must permeate our speech as thoroughly and consistently as the seasoning of salt in a well-blended potluck casserole. When we make kindness, gentleness, patience, and peace a permanent part of our everyday moments, we'll find it easier to say God-honoring words to anyone we encounter throughout our day. Like Dani, the words, "Come back," will flow from our mouths, setting off a chain reaction of hope and restoration.

God longs for us to speak his words to those around us. So how do we improve at speaking words that impart grace and not harm? God's command to Moses includes us as well; "I will help you speak and teach you what to say" (Exod. 4:12).

God has made us managers of all the resources in our world, including the resource of words. When our speech is kind and gracious, we use God's gift of speech to give our listeners a recording of the sound of God's grace.

God put sound in your mouth. Your ability to talk comes from him. All of it: your mouth, your vocal cords, the syllables your mouth and tongue form, the language you speak and think, and God's lavish grace. Honor God by using these gifts for his glory.

> *Thank you, Father, for making my tongue so I am able to speak words that will impact others for the good of your kingdom. Give me wisdom today to speak words that benefit those around me.*

········· LISTENING WITH OPEN EARS ·········

Make a commitment to pay attention to the words you say today. Look for ways to show God's grace and love through your words. Unsure how? Ask the Lord for his guidance.

33

Words of Comfort

Anxiety in a person's heart weighs it down, but a good word makes it glad.

PROVERBS 12:25 NASB

I spotted my friend Lynette halfway across a crowded room. Working my way through a cluster of people, I gave her a hug then reached for her hand. "How are you? I heard you had COVID. Are you okay now?"

"Yes, I'm fine." Then her entire face lit up with a big smile. "Thank you for asking."

Over the last few years, I've asked God to help me do better at showing interest in the people I encounter. I remind myself that my focus should be on them, not me. Whether friend or stranger, store clerk or restaurant server, I've decided to greet people with a smile, a warm and sincere voice, and eye contact. After our initial greeting, I'll ask, "How are you?"—with emphasis on *you.*

As I write this, I fear that you will wonder at my sincerity. Do I really care about the well-being of a stranger? Aren't I concerned that an emotionally needy person might launch into a fifteen-minute monologue about themselves when I don't have the time or energy to listen? That is a risk and yes, I do wonder if others question my motives. But my fears are often unwarranted, for that is not what happens. I'm persistently surprised by the response I get.

"Thank you for asking."

Why does a simple question—"How are you?"—have that level of impact? Is my question so unusual that people are grateful for the asking? Surely not! Doesn't everyone ask, "How are you?" Are people so overloaded with troubles that, when a stranger asks, it means so much?

Yes.

We might know some of the struggles of those closest to us. We hear of crises and catastrophes on social media and news feeds. But as we look out over a sea of people in a theater, shopping mall, or church service, we often have little clue of the hurt and heartache they may be hiding behind plastered smiles. But they know. And inwardly they may be crying out for someone to care.

People I've often judged as unfriendly, reserved, or extremely introverted may actually be struggling to hold their emotions in check while in public. A blank look may be the mask they've secured to hide the inner pain. A friend voiced these conclusions one day when she commented about certain people's perceived unfriendliness at a church function. "We have no idea what other people are facing," she reflected. "They could've just had a fight with their husband or dealt with a rebellious teenager." Or worse. It's hard to look happy and reach out to others, especially to your group's newcomers or strangers, when your own heart is shattered. We all have days when we're doing well just to show up.

None of us are immune to moments of loneliness and abandonment. We're not ready to share with anyone the shame and panic that eat at the lining of our stomachs, how we're about to explode with news we're too wounded to share. But one word, one short sentence of kindness from a friend or stranger, can be enough to give us a lifeline of hope and a semblance of a smile. *Someone recognizes me. Someone values me. Someone cares enough to pause during a busy day to focus on me.*

One good word, one interaction, can make such a difference. It doesn't solve the problem or stop the struggle. But it's like receiving a drink of cool water in a desert wasteland. You don't need an analysis of why you are thirsty. You just need a drink of water. The same is true with the one whose primary emotional goal is to survive. A gentle greeting, a reassurance, or a hand on the shoulder might be the refreshing milk of human kindness that gives the recipient strength and resolve to take a few more steps through their struggle.

> One word, one short sentence of kindness from a friend or stranger, can be enough to give us a lifeline of hope and a semblance of a smile.

I keep thinking I should do more. But two thoughts give me reassurance that, for the moment, I have done enough. First, I don't have to know the other person's struggles. God knows and his Spirit can give me the words they need to hear. One small sentence can do so much good.

Also, we represent the God of all comfort. He's the one in charge of helping the helpless and healing the wounded. He combines my words of concern with a loving gift from another and wise counsel from yet another, and then arranges it all into a love basket from himself. It's his job to help the afflicted. He is the "Father of compassion," as 2 Corinthians 1:3 says, and you and I are part of a select team through whom God passes his love to the ones who struggle.

Say what God gives you to say. If he wants you to do more, he'll let you know. Otherwise, move on to the Lord's next assignment for you, making room for another delivery of comfort.

Say the encouraging words. You may never know how God uses what you say or do to bring comfort, reassurance, and hope into someone's darker season of life. Those words could be the perfect message at the perfect time, known only to that other person and the Holy Spirit.

It can start with something as simple as "How are you?"

Thank you, Lord for hearing me when I cry out for help.
Make me aware of those who need to hear a good word
from you today.

·············· LISTENING WITH OPEN EARS ··············

Who will you intersect with today? Ask God to show you how to express a kind word to those people.

34

Words of Truth

*Timely advice is lovely, like golden apples
in a silver basket.*
PROVERBS 25:11 NLT

*M*y friend Kathy fell in step beside me. "I heard you tell someone
it's been an emotionally intense week for you," she said. "What's
going on?"

I blurted out my story from the past week about a relational mess
I'd been sucked into. I berated myself for my gullibility in getting
pulled into the situation.

Kathy commiserated with me. "That would be difficult to deal
with," she said. Then she gently asked, "What lessons can you learn
from this to carry into your future?"

Confrontation is a tough, scary, and risky job. But someone's got
to do it.

Hearing the truth of what we could do better next time is hard.
Challenging someone else to rise to a higher level of righteousness is
harder. The biblical word *admonish* is not a popular one these days,
for none of us like to hear that we've been less than what we want
people to believe we are.

Certain Bible characters reacted better to truth-bearers in their lives than others. After King David committed adultery with Bathsheba, the prophet Nathan came to him and, using a story to get David's attention, confronted David with the severity of his sin. David immediately confessed and repented (see 2 Sam. 12:1–13). The poignancy of Psalm 51 expresses David's entreaty for God's forgiveness and his admission that he has wronged God more than anyone else.

Hearing the truth of what we could do better next time is hard. Challenging someone else to rise to a higher level of righteousness is harder.

King Asa of a later generation handled confrontation differently. Ruler of Judah for forty-one years, he was a leader who mostly honored God. Yet in the thirty-sixth year of his reign, he made a treaty with a pagan king from a foreign country. The prophet Hanani called him to account for relying on a foreign country rather than on God, concluding with, "For the eyes of the LORD range throughout the earth to strengthen those whose hearts are fully committed to him. You have done a foolish thing, and from now on you will be at war" (2 Chron. 16:9). Angry at Hanani, Asa locked him up in prison and began oppressing some of his people. He never repented, for the Bible says that in his final years, he contracted a disease in his feet and sought help from physicians rather than from God (vv. 10–14).

Despite how others might respond, we need to speak truth into their lives. Kathy's gentle example showed me how fitting words have a better chance of being heard and heeded.

1. Choose the right moment.
Proverbs 25:11 (NLT) calls it "timely advice" and Ecclesiastes 3:1 reminds us that "there is a time for everything, and a season for every activity under the heavens." We hear best when we are ready to hear.

2. Be gentle in what you say.

Proverbs 15:1 says, "A gentle answer turns away wrath, but a harsh word stirs up anger." Our tone of voice and humility of spirit can strongly convey our love and respect for another person while still speaking truth. I think of how Kathy sandwiched her words when she spoke to me. She acknowledged that my situation would be tough for anyone, and then she asked how I would handle the same scenario the next time.

3. People need solutions, not analysis.

How many of us have had people say in so many words, "You know what you did wrong," and then proceed to tell us as if we didn't know? The mistake has already been made, and the person probably already knows how they've blown it. They are seeking how to get out of their mess. The goal of a truth-bearer is to help friends move forward out of the mess, not to become mired in it.

4. Ask questions.

Your questions will give you more understanding and help the other person take ownership of the solution. Then affirm them for the answers they give, building on those answers to give them a solid strategy for moving on.

When we speak words of admonishment or constructive criticism in a spirit of love and a tone of gentleness, we have far better chances of empowering our brother or sister in Christ to move forward and grow in righteousness. We're doing what Ephesians 4:15 says: "Speaking the truth in love, we will grow to become in every respect the mature body of him who is the head, that is, Christ." Encouraging a Christian friend to change agrees they're not where they need to be but gives hope that they don't have to stay there. If you encourage them in a way that propels them forward, you do them, yourself, and the entire body of Christ a huge favor. If one part of the church community becomes stronger, the entire structure gains strength.

I'm deeply grateful for my friend's approach. She didn't criticize or condemn. Instead, she gave wise counsel, something manageable that gave me hope. Her fitting words were as lovely as golden apples set in a silver basket.

Lord, show me the difference between harsh criticism and wise counsel. Help me grow in how I speak the truth in love.

LISTENING WITH OPEN EARS

Do you need to lovingly confront someone about an action they have taken? Speak to them with love and gentleness. If they don't respond well, give them time. Find peace that you have done your part to speak truth laced with love.

35

Idle Chatter

Be very careful, then, how you live—
not as unwise but as wise.
EPHESIANS 5:15

*A*fter Youth Sunday, a day when the youth of our small church led the preaching and singing, I stood at the exit, greeting people as they left. A couple I didn't recognize came toward me. Engaging them in conversation, I discovered they were first-time visitors. I laughed nervously and quipped, "I hope you come back next week. This wasn't our usual kind of service." Unknown to me, the mother of the young man who had preached was standing within earshot and heard every word. She was offended and rightly so.

Words are like feathers spilling from a goose-down pillow outside on a windy day. You can let them out, but you can't stuff them back in. Once words exit our mouths, whether beneficial, harmful, or merely careless, they can reverberate within the echo chambers of the minds and memories of their hearers for years to come.

Speech is a gift, part of how God designed us. But the Lord leaves it to us to choose what we talk about. And whenever we open our mouths, we have an opportunity to invite those around us to stand in wonder once more at God's gift of sound. Words are a precious and

149

powerful resource. If we're careful in the way we spend other resources like time, money, or possessions, and if God calls us to use those earthly resources for eternal purposes, shouldn't we treat words the same way?

Words matter. They have impact. What I say can build up or tear down, encourage or discourage, draw people toward Jesus or draw them toward me and my selfish agendas. Idle talk, like criticism, gossip, sarcasm, or centering the conversation on our accomplishments, joins the noise already present in the room. These blabbed words don't benefit anyone, and they muffle the message people most need to hear.

Words are like feathers spilling from a goose-down pillow outside on a windy day. You can let them out, but you can't stuff them back in.

My heart's desire is to move people toward Jesus. Realizing the potential influence of my words, I want to listen carefully to myself: What words *are* coming out of my mouth? And what word choices could I use instead to bless and build up those around me?

Paul told his readers in the Ephesian church to make "the most of every opportunity, because the days are evil" (Eph. 5:16). The world is already full of demoralizing, crude, senseless, and divisive talk. As Christ followers, our choice of God-honoring, people-respecting talk will stand out in stark contrast. If I truly desire to use all of God's gifts wisely, and I want to make every moment count for the kingdom effort, shouldn't I intentionally measure my words and monitor what I say?

This doesn't mean you and I need to stand on a street corner every day, preaching the gospel message to anyone within earshot. But it does imply that we should think through the impact and influence of our everyday words. Will they advance God's kingdom? Or could they bring harm to God's work, turning people away from the Lord we love? For example, could those who overhear our negative comments about other believers or other churches in our community wonder if Christ followers really love each other after all?

James compared the tongue to an out-of-control fire, saying it's a reckless evil, full of deadly poison (James 3:6–7). You and I know that too well. Though most of us probably don't go around criticizing everyone we meet, we can probably tell countless stories with shame reddening our faces of the times hurtful words have flowed from our mouths. I think of moments when I have blurted out caustic, hurtful words, and I've wondered, *Where did that come from? I didn't want to say that.* Too late! Like tongues of flickering fire, consuming everything along an unpredictable path, once words come out of my mouth, I no longer have control over them.

It makes me want to find the nearest roll of duct tape.

So how can you and I tame the tongue?

First, we can recognize that God's given us a tremendous opportunity to do good and bring him glory through our words. Instead of evaluating whether our past words were good, bad, or irrelevant, let's be proactive. Before you speak, ask yourself, *How will my next sentence bless the person in front of me?*

We also need to acknowledge that the words we say spring out of what is already in our hearts and minds. The Jews of Jesus's day had a hang-up about what foods they could and couldn't eat. They made the mistake of connecting the physical act of eating with someone's spiritual status. Jesus said, however, that a person isn't defiled by what goes into the body but by what comes out of the mouth. Our actions and words spring out of our attitudes and mindsets (Mark 7:18–22). If I want my words to represent Jesus well, I need to look at what I'm thinking. Hurtful words come from corrosive thoughts. Instead, God calls me to set my mind on his agenda (Col. 3:2) and to think about things that are true, noble, and praiseworthy (Phil. 4:8).

Finally, we'll do a better job of speaking edifying words into the lives of others if we first listen to them—if we're "quick to listen, slow to speak" (James 1:19). Turning off our own voices and muting our reactions gives us the chance to listen and gather valuable information about the other person's feelings, thoughts, and current struggles. Our willingness to listen will communicate loud and clear that we care about hearing their voice more than listening to our own.

We have so little time on this earth. Let's make every word count for Jesus.

Lord, remind me through this day to speak words that honor you and benefit others.

LISTENING WITH OPEN EARS

Who might intersect your path in the next two hours? What words can you speak that will bless them and move them closer to Jesus?

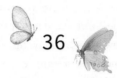

36

Information Overload

There is a time for everything, and a season for
every activity under the heavens . . . a time to be
silent and a time to speak.
ECCLESIASTES 3:1, 7

*Y*ou're too reticent," my brainy fiancé told me.

I didn't know what the word *reticent* meant, but it sounded horrible. His context frustrated me more. "I want to know everything about you, and you aren't forthcoming."

I started talking more about the things that mattered to me. One year later, after we were married, he said, "Get to the end. You talk too much, like my mother."

Dude! Make up your mind.

Aren't the early years of marriage fun?

What a wide spectrum of people God has created, each of us so different from the next! There are more communication styles than colors on the color wheel. Some of us are more relational—shall we say more talkative?—than others. The boys in my high school youth group loved to quote this proverb to the more chatty girls: "Even fools are thought wise if they keep silent" (Prov. 17:28). Some went a step further with the contemporary quote attributed to either Abraham

Lincoln or Mark Twain: "Better to remain silent and be thought a fool than to speak and remove all doubt."

I've learned with my various relationships that each of us has a different style of communication. God has wired some individuals to expend more words by day's end than others. Yet I've also discovered that each of us is wired to *hear* a varying amount of words per day, based on both our personalities and the day's activities. I may have a daily count of twenty thousand words to say, but the person next to me may have already heard an overload of talk. I can show love and respect for those around me by measuring the words I pour into our relationship on any given day.

Some days, after work, Jack would come home with one simple sentence: "My ears are tired." Without asking for the details, I'd know he had heard his limit for the day and the best way I could demonstrate my love for him was to throw away my extra words.

God's Word tells us to love each other deeply, from the heart (1 Peter 1:22). If we're committed to sincerely loving each other, the other person will care about the words we speak, and we will care about the words they hear from us. We will each be mindful of the quality and quantity of our speech. Words are gifts from the hand of our heavenly Father, and God calls us to treat this gift, and the person who hears, as precious in his sight.

> If we're committed to sincerely loving each other, the other person will care about the words we speak, and we will care about the words they hear from us.

Speaking and listening are an everyday balancing game, especially when we sense the person before us doesn't have the need to talk as much as we do but we still have important things to discuss. I'm still working at finding the balance between enough and too much in my marriage communication. I've learned to notice what my husband is busy doing before I jump into a detailed account of my latest escapade. Of the two of us, I have a bigger warehouse of words to use up by the end of the day. I problem solve by talking out loud and I need a sounding board. We call those moments "yes, dear" conversations. I go to my husband. "I need to talk something out. I don't want fix-it solutions. I don't want blow-offs or criticisms. I just need to talk. So, anything I say, please respond with, 'Yes, dear.'"

"Yes, dear."

It goes from there. If I had an ice-cream cone for every time he says "Yes, dear" during the conversation, I'd go into sugar shock. Usually by the end of my processing, we're laughing so hard my issue doesn't seem so serious. He's allowed me to hit a release value that siphons the stress of the moment. Many times, I've come up for air midway and said, "Would you tell me what you think?"

He needs to talk too, and he needs me to listen, whether he's telling me in detail about a news article or his heart concern over issues in our church family. In those moments, I need to hit the pause button and let him talk, uninterrupted. We've learned to give each other the space and freedom to talk.

But how do you handle someone who hasn't been sensitive enough to check your audio fatigue before they speak? The person who seems to have a reserve tank of oxygen because they can talk for ten minutes without taking a breath. Before you label them as one of Abraham Lincoln's fools, pay attention to what they're saying. Think of who stands before you and ask yourself, *What is this person normally like? What are they going through right now?*

Some people may be habitual or conscripted listeners. They've listened to other people all day and they still have eighteen thousand words left in their warehouse, so they need to use them up—now. Others, particularly the elderly, have spent all day alone. Their vocal cords need exercise, and they have the need to be heard. Still others, I've found, are socially uncomfortable and feel compelled to fill the silence with nervous chatter.

How do we respond?

"Love is patient, love is kind," Paul wrote to the Corinthian church (1 Cor. 13:4). He told the Colossian church to bear with one another or, as one translation says, "make allowance for each other's faults" (Col. 3:13 NLT). Just as I rely on God to set aside my need to talk when my husband comes home tired, I can ask God to renew my strength of hearing so I can be attentive to the one who needs someone to listen. If God can do anything—and we know he can—then he will give me the patience and endurance I need.

Part of unity within the body of Christ is learning to accept each other where we're at while patiently strengthening each other to become what God wants us to be. As others accept my warts, quirks, and failings, so I also accept them as they are. And that includes how we talk.

Lord, show me when I need to listen more than speak. Help me be patient and understanding toward those who speak more words than what I feel able to hear.

·········· LISTENING WITH OPEN EARS ··········

What conversations in your life drag on more than you would like? What does that person want you to know about them? How can you show God's grace and gently guide them toward becoming more like Jesus?

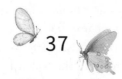

37

Unwholesome Talk

*Do not let any unwholesome talk come out of
your mouths, but only what is helpful for building
others up according to their needs, that it may
benefit those who listen.*

EPHESIANS 4:29

hen my two girls were in middle school, they did not like riding the school bus. Since part of the route wove through a rough neighborhood, I worried that they were being harassed by students from that area.

"It's not that," one daughter told me. "Mom, there's so much bad language on the bus and the bus driver does nothing to stop it." Her face grew troubled. "I don't like hearing those words. They stay in my mind for hours later and then I'm tempted to use them—and I know I shouldn't."

I had taught my girls, as I had been taught, that the Bible teaches against vulgarity. We used Ephesians 4:29 as a guiding light whenever the words threatened to move from our brains to our mouths: "Do not let any unwholesome talk come out of your mouth . . ."

Foul words are unwholesome. They don't add any benefit to a conversation; in fact, they're rather uncreative in conveying what we really want to say. And even the most blameless person among us finds it tempting to let those words fly when sucked into anger. That should be a big clue that the words aren't wise. Anger can destroy relationships, and words spoken in anger can act as battle-axes. The uncontrolled anger is the core problem.

But as a teen and now as a mom, I hesitated to use this particular verse exclusively as a proof text for what our family started calling "worty dirds" (a play on the phrase "dirty words," meant to lighten our girls' distress). It's easy to feel pride when I don't use any of the language on a short list of despicable word choices. Then my conscience pricks me. Aren't there other ways to use words that tear others down instead of building them up?

We can't limit unwholesome talk to a few banned words. That becomes a legalistic mindset. If I don't say a short list of five certain words, then I'm good with God, right? It's not that simple. Word choice is as much about intent, arrangement of words, and time appropriateness as it is about the specific words. Ephesians 4:29 provides an alternative to unwholesome words: Choose helpful and beneficial words that speak of God's grace to our listeners.

> We can't limit unwholesome talk to a
> few banned words. It's not that simple.

My word-nerd bent kicked in recently. I looked up Ephesians 4:29 in other Bible versions to see how they translated the word *unwholesome*. Other translations say *corrupt, evil, dirty,* and *bad.* Then I checked the Greek word for *unwholesome*. It literally means "rotten, as in a form of decay."[4]

Wow. That struck hard.

Vulgar words are words of decay because their meanings convey anger, derision, or condemnation. But I know too well that my words

---

4. *Vine's Expository Dictionary*, 17th ed. (1966), under "sapros."

of gossip, criticism, or sarcasm can be equally destructive. Even stony silence speaks a strong message. My goal should be to actively, intentionally choose words that strengthen the people around me instead of making them wither, break down, and yes, even rot.

I don't remember how I answered my children about keeping those corrosive words out of their heads. If I were speaking to them today, further along in my understanding about the impact of rotten words, I'd advise my girls to focus on saying beneficial words to others. I would encourage them to look at others, no matter who they are, as people created and loved by God and in need of his grace. Most of all, I would work harder to model the right kind of strong language in our own home—words that strengthen, build up, and reinforce each person's individual relationship with God. I'd aim to have conversations that didn't bring decay or cause their love for Jesus to fade or break down.

Words have meaning, but the intention behind our words matters as much as the actual choice of words. The broader meaning behind Ephesians 4:29 is so important, it's worth looking more closely at several types of rotting words in the next few chapters and exploring how we can stand up against language that threatens to tear us down.

In the meantime, I'm recommitting myself to the words of Psalm 19:14: "May these words of my mouth and this meditation of my heart be pleasing in your sight, LORD, my Rock and my Redeemer."

Will you join me?

Lord, would you prick my spirit every time an unwholesome word wants to pass from my mind to my mouth? Would you also give me an alternate way to express myself, a way that would strengthen the person standing before me?

LISTENING WITH OPEN EARS

Do an internal search on rotten words that litter your vocabulary—whether vulgarities, gossip, sarcasm, or criticism. Spend time praying that the Lord will help you delete those words from daily conversations.

38

Complaints

*And my God will meet all your needs according to
the riches of his glory in Christ Jesus.*
PHILIPPIANS 4:19

*A*n older church friend patiently listened to my over-the-top description of dreading my first visit to a new ophthalmologist. With my complicated eyesight issues, eye exams truly are uncomfortable. I'd rather go to the dentist. And my previous life experience of needing to find a new ophthalmologist within days of moving to a new town tells me doctors who are new to my case might not understand the severity of my eye disorder.

"It's so hard," I finished my story with a melodramatic whimper.

She didn't flinch. "You want cheese with that whine?"

We were both being lighthearted, but grumbling is not always funny. Her humorous comment portrays the unpleasantness of listening to a grumbler. One day, I rejoiced to someone at the good rain we'd had the night before after months with no rain. She didn't smile. Instead, she said, "It wasn't enough." *Oh, come on!*

How did I respond? I grumbled to my husband about the ungrateful people in my life.

Unless we're reclusive, we hear grumbling every day. And if we care to admit it, we've grumbled too. *I'm not grumbling, I'm observing,* my husband and I will say to each other. Call it what it is. If we're showing discontent with our current circumstances, projecting a negative outcome, and refusing to look at the positives and possibilities, we're not giving life or God a fair chance.

God takes grumbling seriously—especially if it's questioning his goodness and care for us. He showed the Israelites awesome displays of power when he led them out of Egypt, parting the Red Sea so they could escape the pursuing Egyptian army on dry land. Three days later, when they couldn't find water in the desert, they started to grumble (Exod. 15:24). God provided the water but gave them a warning that they needed to stay faithful to him.

> God takes grumbling seriously—
> especially if it's questioning his
> goodness and care for us.

Only a few days later, they grumbled again, this time about food (Exod. 16:1–3), and God provided manna for them to eat. The grumbling continued—about food, water, Moses's leadership, God's decisions, and the difficult task of conquering Canaan. The discontent spread like a disease until, at one point, the entire community opposed Moses (Num. 14:1–4). God was not happy. He brought a plague of judgment upon the Israelites that killed 14,700 people (Num. 16:49).

I wonder how I would've reacted if I were in the middle of that crowd. After all, isn't lack of water or food a serious thing? I complain if avocados go up in price or milk is out of stock. Why does God react so strongly to grumbling even if it's for what we see as a legitimate concern? Because, at its core, grumbling is a failure to trust God. Even when he has proven himself in the past through awesome displays of power to be the Provider God.

Jesus confronted the disciples with this truth when they struck out across the Sea of Galilee and were dismayed that they'd forgotten to bring bread. He used their lapse as a teachable moment to warn them about the influence of the Pharisees. They didn't get it. They fixated on having no bread. Jesus said to them, "Do you still not understand? Don't you remember the five loaves for the five thousand, and how many basketfuls you gathered? Or the seven loaves for the four thousand, and how many basketfuls you gathered?" (Matt. 16:9–10). If Jesus, as Lord of the universe, could feed five thousand families with one boy's lunch, wouldn't he be able to take care of twelve men on a boat?

I still find myself grumbling about the silly stuff and the not-so-silly stuff. I may think I'm being lighthearted, but my words taunt God's care for me and cause others to question his goodness.

How do we change our style of speech?

We pray that God will send out a warning when we're tempted to utter or think negative thoughts. We push back the grumpy grumbles by reviewing what God has done for us in the past. We commit ourselves once again to trusting the God who has provided before and who will do it again. And if the things we want to grumble about are the grumblers? God is fully capable of taking care of them too. Relinquish those people to the Lord and stay faithful in your commitment to trust him.

We can do more. We can boldly counter grumbling with positive messages that show our trust in God. Yes, we'll get pushback from those who persist in looking at what's lacking. But bystanders will hear and appreciate that no one needs to stay in the land of discontent.

"How was your appointment?" my friend later asked me.

"It was fine. The doctor is great!" While it would have been truthful to mention the minor snag I encountered with the clinic's finance department (which did get resolved), I didn't need to put that information into the airwaves. Instead, I chose to focus on the equally true report about the kindness and competence of my new doctor.

One step, one sentence at a time, we can replace the grumbling with gratitude. When we do, we help others hear what it's like to trust God in everything.

Forgive me, Father, for the times I show a lack of trust in your care for me by grumbling. Warn me when I'm about to whine so I don't infect others with an ungrateful spirit.

LISTENING WITH OPEN EARS

Make a list of ten things God has provided for you or done for you in the last day. The next time you want to grumble about life, look at your list to remind yourself that God is powerful enough to take care of you.

Loving Discipline

Start children off on the way they should go, and
even when they are old they will not turn from it.
PROVERBS 22:6

Seeking a peaceful place to do some computer work, I went to our local library. All was quiet and I tuned out the normal noises, like activity at the checkout desk and patrons walking past my seat. I hardly noticed a man and his small son entering the bathroom across the aisle from me. Once the door closed, though, my concentration shattered.

In a loud voice, the man proceeded to chew out his son for an undefined infraction. I don't remember the specific accusations, but I do know they dealt more with the boy's character than his actions, and one action was broadened into a character flaw. I cringed with every harsh word, wishing I could bolt into the men's bathroom to stop the tirade. I heard a barrage of accusations. *You always do this. You're no good. Why don't you ever listen to me? You'll never amount to anything.* If I wanted to crawl under my desk at the vitriol, I can only imagine how that little boy felt.

I grieved for that father. I grieved for any past and present moments that had forged such an emotional reaction from a tired, stressed-out man who may have never learned good parenting skills. I grieved for his future, because once those words left his mouth, he no longer had control over the potential long-term damage they could have on his relationship with his son. Even an apology would not fully heal the memory etched on that child's soul.

Wise King Solomon's book of Proverbs is a great parenting guide. In a long series of two-phrase, easy-to-remember proverbs, Solomon spells out specific ways his son can make right choices rooted in a respectful fear of God. Near the top of the list is this command: "Listen, my son, to your father's instruction and do not forsake your mother's teaching" (Prov. 1:8).

Children can't do what is right if they don't know what is right. They must be taught. A mistake many parents make, including myself, is to only tell our children when they've blown it instead of instructing them about the right choice before they make the wrong one.

I'm wondering how that father could have handled his son's antics better. My storytelling mind concocts an alternate ending. The father did the right thing by taking his son into a private space. From there, he could have knelt before his son, put his hand on the boy's shoulder, and said, "Son, I don't know how well I've explained this to you in the past. But here's what you did. That is wrong. You should not do that. And when I tell you to do something, you must obey me. Because you didn't obey me, there are consequences. Since God made me to be your dad, God gave me the job to make sure you learn to do the right thing." And at that point, the dad would have administered the discipline that best suited his child and then hugged the boy, reaffirming his love for him.

Nice story. But I'm smart and honest enough to know that every parent has their bad moments. Many of us have said hurtful words that we regret for the rest of our lives. And not just to our children either. Degrading words, no matter who says them or who hears them, seep into a person's psyche like the poison of a tick that causes the lingering effects of Lyme disease.

I was a witness to what happened that day behind the closed door of a public bathroom. How much more happens behind the fences and doors of homes that we don't know about? I'm increasingly aware of the stress and heartache parents carry in today's world, and of the number of parents who emerged from dysfunctional families where they were broken and browbeaten and never learned any other way to parent.

Degrading words, no matter who says them or who hears them, seep into a person's psyche like the poison of a tick that causes the lingering effects of Lyme disease.

What's the solution? How do we diffuse the power of demeaning words?

I've heard it said that it takes ten affirmations of praise to countermand one negative criticism. If we're going to rescue our children from the effect of demeaning words, we've got a lot of work ahead of us. So, what can we do? When we encounter children God has placed in our corner of the world, we can let them hear words of love, affirmation, praise, interest, and attention. They need it. Desperately. You and I may never know what they've heard in the last half hour, whether from a parent, an older sibling, a critical grandma, an overworked teacher, or a school bully. Every child gives us the opportunity to feed their starving ears with words they need to hear: "You are important. You are smart. You are worthwhile. God loves you."

Who are the children who can hear your voice? Some are permanent residents in your heart, others flit in and out, and still others are onetime contacts. But they all need spoken reminders that God loves them and that he is the source of truth and guidance for right living. Through our attention, we can drop wise words into their laps, quietly redirect bad behavior, and model how humans should treat each other.

By pausing for a few seconds to acknowledge a child, we may be giving a parent the time they need to regroup, breathe deeply, and re-commit themselves to doing a better job at instructing their child. It's a win-win for everyone.

> *Lord, I commit myself to speak words of love and affirmation to the beaten-down people in my life, especially the children. Help me do that.*

LISTENING WITH OPEN EARS

Which children hear your voice? What defamatory voices are they hearing? What words can you say to diffuse the damaging words they hear?

40

Rumors

Whoever would foster love covers over an offense,
but whoever repeats the matter
separates close friends.
PROVERBS 17:9

*D*id you know . . . ?"

My husband's blood pressure always went up when his administrative assistant used those words. He braced himself.

"Viola died this afternoon."

Jack's tension increased. This wasn't the first time his assistant had passed on false information. "I just came from the hospital. Viola is very much alive."

There was a short silence. "Oh dear. I guess I'd better call back the ten people I've already told."

You think?

While sad and exasperating, the spread of that misinformation had no long-term effects. But another time, a neighbor in that long-ago era of our ministry work told us a church member had problems with alcohol. In all the years we knew this sweet, gentle, godly man and his wife, we never saw any trace of an addiction. Yet through the years, that possibility was implanted in our minds, and we wondered—*does he?*

That's what gossip does. It tosses poison into the well of a relationship and has the potential to put a wedge between friends. Idle talk about other people's affairs, usually with a negative bent, influences others to filter their interactions with those people because they now wonder if what they've heard is true.

I'm sure our neighbor meant well. He probably thought we needed to know about our church member's possible addiction; perhaps we'd be able to help. The "need-to-know" marker is a good yardstick to use when we're deciding whether to share information, but it has its drawbacks. Our human minds can easily rationalize why someone else "needs to know." Well-meaning people often confuse gossip with prayer requests. So often I hear friends say, after telling me juicy details about another's private life, "We can't do anything, but we can pray!" I would love to retort, "*Are* you praying?"

When we pass on private details, we might inadvertently add to information overload. We are an information-driven society. "Knowledge is power," we say. We forget that the wrong kind of knowledge in less than capable hands can lead to the wrong kind of power. And too much knowledge can overload the power grid, burdening people's spirits in ways God never intended. Worse yet, like my husband's assistant's report, our information might be wrong.

"Whoever would foster love covers over an offense, but whoever repeats the matter separates close friends," says Proverbs 17:9. I like the way the New International Version translates that first sentence in a way other English translations don't. The word *foster* means to promote the growth and development of something. As lovers of God, our goal is to promote and nurture love—between us and God, us and others, and between other people besides ourselves. When we're tempted to pass on news about a third party, especially about their weaknesses, poor choices, or struggles, we need to ask ourselves, *How will talking about this nurture love within my circle of people?*

That would be a game changer in the life of any Christian community.

Refusing to start or spread rumors is a first step toward ending not-so-loving talk about a third party. But what about when gossip runs circles around my group? I can close my eyes to unsightly things; it's harder to close my ears. It would be rude to clap my hands over my ears and stalk out of a room. It's not always effective to scold or question someone for sharing information we don't want to hear. Besides, sometimes the words get out before we can stop them, and the damage is done.

> We need to ask ourselves, *How will talking about this nurture love within my circle of people?*

What do we do then?

I've learned to use various responses when someone wants to share negative or unreliable stories with me.

"I imagine there's a lot more we don't know, so perhaps it's best not to come to any conclusion without more information."

"My brain is stuffed right now. If you don't mind, I think this is information I don't need to know, especially right now. Can we shift our talk to other things?"

"Great idea about the need for prayer. Let's stop and pray right now. Would you like to lead us?"

And my favorite? Often community people saw me, the pastor's wife, as someone "in the know," so they would seek me out to get the latest on a person's situation. I would smile and say, "I know much more than I should tell." That worked every time. My "latest development" seeker would raise a hand and say, "Fair enough. I won't press."

The next time you hear or feel tempted to speak damaging words about another person, think about 1 Peter 1:22, which encourages us to love each other deeply from the heart. If you have deep love for someone, will you speak words that put them in a bad light? Or will you want to protect them? What words will best show your faithful love and respect for them?

Let's be game changers. Let's speak about others as if they are part of our inner circle of friends: people we sincerely love, care about, and want to see become the best they can be.

> *Lord, I invite your Holy Spirit to show me when I'm about to say untrue or unkind words about another person. Give me wisdom to know how to respond when I hear gossip about others.*

·············· LISTENING WITH OPEN EARS ··············

Read Philippians 4:8. Think about the things you have heard and said so far today, especially about other people. How do they stack up compared to the list of attributes in this verse?

41

Blame Games

Set your minds on things above,
not on earthly things.
COLOSSIANS 3:2

When Jack was a pastor in rural Kansas, he often traveled to the big city 130 miles away to visit older parishioners in the hospital. He would come home late, past our children's bedtime. Missing him, I turned on the front porch light one night, remembering the tagline from the Motel 6 commercial about leaving the light on. I wanted him to know someone was looking forward to seeing him.

He was not happy. "Why are you wasting so much electricity?" he accused. "I don't need the light. I open the garage door; that gives me the light I need."

I tried to explain, but that made things worse. He continued, "You're pointing out how late I am. The neighbors will notice the front porch light and wonder why I'm out so late."

I should have realized these words came from an overtired, overworked, overstressed man. I should have intuited that he needed my protection of his private life, and the best way to love him was to leave the light off. But I've never handled false accusations well. Something inside me wants to prove that I have good intentions. I want to persuade the accuser that those things aren't true and how could they think such things of me? Don't they know me better than that? And I've had moments of retaliation where I level the playing field with my own accusations.

The gospel record tells me Jesus heard plenty of false accusations. Religious leaders constantly dogged his heels: *He associates with the wrong kind of people. He is working for the enemy. He is too full of himself, thinking he is someone great when he is just the kid next door from the carpenter's shop.* The accusations mounted as his enemies looked for ways to get rid of him. At his kangaroo court trial before the governor Pilate, the Jewish leaders accused him of causing riots, inciting the people to turn against the Roman government, and claiming to be the Messiah.

They had that last one correct, at least partly so. He *was* the Messiah.

It wasn't fair.

How did Jesus handle those false accusations? He said nothing.

Jesus! My inner voice screams when I read these passages. *It's not true. Defend yourself. Set them straight.* I know how I would want to react. Prideful human nature wants to show others we're not as evil as they think. We become zealous for the truth, and we want our accusers to accept that truth. I don't like anyone being at odds with me. *This person is reasonable*, I think. *If they give me a chance to explain why I did what I did, of course they'll say, "Oh yes. I understand now."*

Why did Jesus remain silent? Didn't these people need to know he was the Messiah?

Consider this. If Jesus had succeeded in persuading his accusers of his innocence, he would never have made it to the cross. God used those false accusations to motivate Pilate to sentence Jesus to death so he could die for the guilt of the world. Jesus knew that was his mission. For the sake of his Father's goal, for the bigger picture, he kept quiet. "For the joy set before him he endured the cross, scorning its shame, and sat down at the right hand of the throne of God" (Heb. 12:2).

If Jesus had defended himself, more than likely the Jews would not have replied with, "Oh, we get it now. We're cool. You're off the hook." You and I know what happens when we get sucked in to justifying ourselves. It has the adverse effect of making our accusers angrier and more vicious. Pride tempts us to let the emotion of the moment fill our mouths with words that have devastating results. The heightened, dragged-out emotionalism was a distraction Jesus didn't need at that moment. If he had argued back, no matter how he handled it, his words could have been twisted to validate apparent guilt. As long as he remained silent, he remained blameless, and his accusers hung themselves with their own words.

> For the sake of his Father's goal, for the bigger picture, Jesus kept quiet.

Pausing to deal with false accusations takes time and energy. It's hard to allow others to believe we're wrong. But we can follow Jesus's example of remaining silent, not answering or returning the blame, by keeping our eyes on God's big-picture plan. We may need to look for kernels of truth and talk to the Lord about what he thinks we need to change. After that, we slough off the false claims of our accusers and keep looking to Jesus. He—not our accusers—is the one in charge of perfecting our faith (Heb. 12:2).

The next time someone accuses you falsely, listen without responding. Then ask God to help you focus on his eternal plan rather than earthly matters. Your choice to not respond will show your accusers for what they are and will speak to bystanders of your integrity, righteousness, and commitment to Jesus.

Lord, give me the strength to control my words when someone falsely accuses me. Remind me of the work you have for me to do right now so I can stay focused on your purposes and your values.

·················· **LISTENING WITH OPEN EARS** ··················

Have you accused someone recently? Ask God's forgiveness and, if appropriate, go to that person and apologize for what you said. You might try saying, "That wasn't helpful to either of us, and it didn't need to be said." Ask the Lord to give you the words you need to affirm the person standing before you.

42

Testimonies

Live such good lives among the pagans that,
though they accuse you of doing wrong,
they may see your good deeds and glorify God
on the day he visits us.
1 PETER 2:12

I stood at the counter of our local convenience market, holding my gift card midair. Why wasn't it working?

The clerk swiped the card. It still didn't work. She used the trick of wrapping a plastic bag around the card edge and swiped again. Nothing.

Another clerk joined her, a woman whose daughter attended our church's after-school program. The three of us continued trying to solve my gift card problem by calling the regional office and working through my phone app, but with no success.

My frustration mounted and overflowed into my voice and expression. "Why isn't this working?" I said as I sent a penetrating look at one clerk. Then I instantly lowered my head to look at the phone app, ashamed. As the pastor's wife in one of the bigger churches in our small community, I'd worked hard to build relationships, be friendly and caring, slip in words about Jesus, and tell people I was praying for them. I wanted to do more than pass out invitations to church events; I wanted to model how a Christian should live. Despite all my efforts, I often felt like no one noticed, that I was accomplishing nothing.

And now I was losing my cool in a convenience store.

I looked up from my phone. "I'm sorry. I shouldn't be so frustrated. Please, I'm not angry at either of you. You're as trapped in the middle about this card as I am."

"We know," the second woman said. "We know you, and we know what you're like. You wouldn't treat us like that."

Someone *had* noticed. People *were* watching how I lived my life for Jesus. And it took a tense moment, even with a wobble of frustration, to show them how I handled conflict.

Hearing words about Jesus isn't enough to convince others that faith in Jesus is the better idea. Those around us will see the validity of our message when our words are linked to a life of kindness, grace, forgiveness, gratitude, and daily trust in God. Our character becomes the structure that holds the gospel message we long to convey. But if our earthly life doesn't match up to our heavenly message, our lives become nothing more than a house of cards that collapses when circumstances get tough, crushing both our faith and our message.

> Those around us will see the validity of our message when our words are linked to a life of kindness, grace, forgiveness, gratitude, and daily trust in God.

Ruth, an ancestor of King David, showed that character counts. A Moabite by birth, she'd married a man from Judah. When he died, she was determined to return to his land with her mother-in-law. She articulated her commitment to the God of Israel when she said to Naomi, "Your people will be my people and your God my God" (Ruth 1:16).

Ruth proved her new faith in God by her actions. She entered a country where foreigners were not welcome. She moved in with her widowed mother-in-law and cared for her. She lowered herself to gather leftover harvest grain as only the poorest of the poor would do. She submitted to the Jewish custom of marrying a member of Naomi's family so the family inheritance could be preserved. Ruth's actions defined her character so well that Boaz praised her: "All the people of my town know that you are a woman of noble character" (Ruth 3:11).

You may feel like you're not as noble as Ruth. You know the moments you've wobbled, even stumbled. You and I know the times we've talked badly about others, used foul language that would make our adult children blush, and grumbled about circumstances that, in the scheme of eternity, don't really matter. We've put words in the air that have been more blather than blessing to those who heard them. Maybe you've felt tension from those who think your life choices are strange. And you fear that the only times they'll notice your faith in Jesus are the moments when you don't live up to it.

Don't give up. If you are determined to actively trust God even when life gets tough, others will see that you handle problems differently than the way the world does. Deep down, they see the good you do and how you are seeking to be better. They do notice how you depend on God to be your strength and comfort.

They may not understand it. They may accuse you of false motives because to them, fitting your life choices into the world's model of life is like putting square pegs in round holes. But they are listening and watching. And as 1 Peter 2:12 tells us, on the day Christ returns—and hopefully before—they will glorify God for what he has done in your life.

Those unsure about Jesus need to hear the message we have to share. But they also need to see the results and benefits of a commitment to Christ. When you develop that "noble character," they will see that belief in Jesus is worth the effort and it is the best way—the only way—to live.

*Lord, help me represent you well, in both the words I
choose to say and the actions I choose to do. Open the
ears of those around me so they can hear your message
through the way I live.*

·················· LISTENING WITH OPEN EARS ··················

Who do you plan to see today who may not have a strong relationship
with Jesus? Start praying now that God will help you model a godly
character in front of that person.

43

Instruction

And the things you have heard me say in the
presence of many witnesses entrust to reliable
people who will also be qualified to teach others.
2 TIMOTHY 2:2

The classroom of fifth graders fell silent. The captain of our class softball team had chosen me to be the catcher, and that did not sit well with the class. One girl finally spoke up. "Karen can't be catcher. Our fourth-grade teacher would never let her do that. She can't see."

"Karen can do anything she wants to," Mrs. Winn said. "Don't any of you forget that."

I never did.

I also never forgot the words I heard five years later from my high school geometry teacher. I had no trouble memorizing the definitions and axioms that governed the subject of geometry. But when we started to apply those principles in word problems, I was lost. I went to my teacher for help.

His response? "With your vision problems, I can understand why you can't do geometry."

Message received. I can do anything—except geometry. A teacher had said so. To this day, I may not remember the difference between an acute and an isosceles triangle, but I remember Mr. Battle's words: "You can't."

No wonder the writer of the book of James says that not many should become teachers (3:1). I get it. A teacher is supposed to know more than the student. They are an authority in their area of expertise and are seen as more besides. We feel whatever a teacher says must be true, whether or not it has anything to do with their subject. When my daughter taught English as a second language to international students at an American university, she and her colleagues were often the first point of contact for students new to the United States who would seek out advice beyond the classroom topic for even such things as recommendations for cold medication. They respected the teachers and viewed them as knowledgeable resources. Whatever words a teacher says carry extra weight because, well, they're a teacher!

The problem is that teachers are fallible human beings. A teacher's tongue is a major tool of their trade. And, oh, how tongues can get us into trouble quickly, as James points out. Faster than the flames of a forest fire and more lethal than the poison of a king cobra, in one sentence, the tongue can shred a child's psyche, inject self-doubt, and destroy belief in God. One parent told me how they had raised their child to believe in God, but a high school English teacher made such a compelling case for evolution one day that the child turned from God completely and never came back. Kids can blow off their parents as not knowing what they're talking about, but whatever a teacher says *must* be true.

Yet we need teachers who will guide with objective wisdom and truth. We need instructors in the public forum who see their job as an opportunity to both impart knowledge and influence behavior, preparing their students to make their world a better place. We need good teachers, mentors, and Bible study leaders in the church as well. Parents need to act as godly teachers of their children. Older Christian women, by their lives and words, are to teach the younger women (Titus 2:3–5).

Many Bible passages urge us to teach the next generation about God so that faith doesn't die out in our corner of the world. We are to teach our children, and others' children as well, so that the doctrine about God stays intact. We're to teach each other so we grow in our faith. The word *disciple* used in the New Testament means "learner," and Jesus told his followers to go and make disciples (Matt. 28:19). If we are making disciples, we're serving in the role of a teacher.

But wait. There's that meddlesome verse from James 3:1 that says not many should become teachers. *Maybe others should do the teaching. Not me! I might ruin a child's or another believer's life.* None of us want to slip and make a stray comment that destroys someone's trust in God like that math teacher leveled my confidence to study geometry.

Teaching comes with risks and responsibilities. We shouldn't approach any task thinking only of the glory and not the grime. James was asking us, as Jesus did, to count the cost. If you choose to teach anyone about Jesus, whether formally or informally, realize the risk you are taking. Mentoring anyone in the faith means you will need to monitor your life even more carefully, because others are watching what you do after the instruction is over. They're listening within and beyond your area of expertise. And if you teach in a classroom setting, your words, whether on or off topic, will slip into your students' backpacks as they exit the classroom door.

The best way to succeed at teaching others about Jesus is to have the attitude James described later in his book, that we carry a spirit of humility into our daily lives and our instruction (see 3:13–16). We don't know it all. A Bible teacher does not have the final word. They are merely a guide who points their students toward Jesus, the Master Teacher who *is* the final Word. Our job, as influencers for Jesus, is to say through our words and actions, "This is Jesus. Listen to him."

> The best way to succeed at teaching others about Jesus is to carry a spirit of humility into our daily lives.

Yes, we need good, dedicated, humble, and loving influencers. Whether they have an official role in a public school, private school, or

Sunday school, or they act as a daily "guide by your side" within the faith community or the privacy of their homes, we need people who will speak God's love and the hope of God's promises into the lives of those who come behind us. As we teach, we need to utterly rely on God, knowing we are imperfect, but he is not. He can work through us to speak words into the lives of others, words that motivate them for good and for God's glory throughout the rest of their lives.

Lord, others need to hear about your ways. Take away my fear that I might speak your truths in an unworthy way. Speak your words through me in such a way that others will want to follow you more closely.

LISTENING WITH OPEN EARS

Do you know a Christian who is a teacher in a public school? Pause to pray for them, that even though they're not formally teaching Christian principles, God will guide them to lead by example and speak life through their words and actions.

44

Gentle Words

A gentle answer deflects anger, but harsh words
make tempers flare.
PROVERBS 15:1 NLT

I heard the story from others before my husband told me.

Jack attended a school board meeting where a group of angry parents had gathered to voice heated and varying opinions over the board's decision to incorporate a "values-free" sex education curriculum. Emotions overtook logic and tempers flared. A lot of well-meaning parents hurled personal accusations, and the meeting started to swirl out of control.

Then Jack spoke. His calm, articulate voice pointed out that "values-free" still teaches values. He then encouraged the crowd, "Let's teach our kids to do what is right."

Silence.

And the meeting ended shortly after that.

Jack's words acted like a blanket thrown over a blazing fire. His moderated voice, which spoke reason and encouragement, diffused the anger in the room. When I heard the story, I thought of Proverbs 15:1 and how gentle answers have the power to deflect anger. *The Bible is right!*

It sounds counterintuitive. Many of us have been led to believe that sometimes the only way to get someone's attention is to shout above everyone else. That's the only language some people understand, so fight fire with fire, right? After all, we don't want to appear weak or wishy-washy.

But gentle responses work because they are the stuff that meekness is made of—strength under control. When it comes to heated discussions, fighting fire with fire only makes a bigger flame.

At first, a gentle answer is hard, because it's so easy to get sucked into the emotion of the moment. Pride enters the arena, and we want to convince the other person how right we are. Often, my desire to persuade my opponent of my point of view sprays a hard veneer over my words. Then to my dismay, instead of backing down, the other person will respond in kind. Harsh words either cause spontaneous combustion or kindle a smoldering silent fire within my listener that will burst into flame at another unguarded moment.

> Gentle responses work because they are the stuff that meekness is made of—strength under control.

When confronted about a harsh approach, I've heard good people say, "That's the way I am. I'm blunt. Other people should know that and not be offended." But the Bible is right. Harsh words will stir up anger in the best of us. The burden of preventing damage from harsh words begins with the person who says them. If we say, "That is the way I am," we're not giving God a chance to change us. That may be the way we are, but what does God want us to be?

God wants us to be peacemakers. For as James 3:18 says, peacemakers accomplish a lot more in the name of righteousness than insensitive words ever will. How do we create peace through gentle responses?

1. Pray.

If you tend to speak too bluntly or let your emotions rule over reason, ask God to prick your conscience when those sharp words bristle on the edge of your tongue. Let him fill your mouth with his words and attitudes instead.

2. Think of the person before you.

I admit, sometimes I get carried away with my own agenda. When I think how my words might hurt my husband or children, I ask myself, *Do I really want to hurt this person I love so much? How can I use what I say to show my love and respect for this person I say I love?*

3. Do only what you can do.

Sometimes your soft answer will have no effect. No matter what you say, how you respond, or what you do, someone gets angry. Sometimes people may not want to hear the truth. Think of what happened to the apostle Paul. When he came to Jerusalem to worship at the temple, his enemies stirred up a riot and Paul was arrested. He asked for permission to speak to the angry crowd (see Acts 21:27–40). At first the crowd settled down, but then Paul said words they didn't want to hear, and the crowd exploded in worse anger than before (22:21–22).

This same Paul tells us, "If it is possible, as far as it depends on you, live at peace with everyone" (Rom. 12:18). The pivotal phrase is "as far as it depends on you." If you've prayed and spoken to the best of your ability in a kind voice, and your listener still responds in anger, the fault is theirs, not yours.

4. Try again.

As you change, others may not be used to the new you. If you slip, especially with those who know you best, have the humility to say, "I was wrong in how I spoke to you. I'm sorry. Will you give me another chance to say what I'm trying to say in a different way?" They may still be too angry to accept your apology, but they will know that you want to be gentle. The next time, they'll be more willing to listen.

Our world is full of harsh, unforgiving, and unkind words. Our gentle, loving words can act as fire control. They won't put out every fire, but our reasoned, calm responses can help keep anger and animosity from spreading any further.

> *Father God, help me speak kind words during tense moments. Give me the words I need to bring peace.*

LISTENING WITH OPEN EARS

Listen to the conversations around you. What examples of gentle responses can you imitate? How would you rewrite the harsh, insensitive words you hear? How could you incorporate that style into your own speech?

45

Breaking News

*First, I thank my God through Jesus Christ
for all of you, because your faith is being reported
all over the world.*
ROMANS 1:8

*D*id you hear about the little church in rural Illinois that sheltered seventy people and four dogs from a blizzard?

I did.

Truth. Jack was the pastor of that rural Illinois church, so I had a front-row seat for the action. But I also witnessed how the story went viral as people told what happened through word of mouth, social media, and into the ears and keyboards of regional newspapers. Forever, there will be groups of people who remember the Thanksgiving Blizzard of 2018 not for its ferocity but for the power of God to save and shelter stranded travelers from the brunt of a winter storm.

Several years earlier, the fire department of Warren County had approached our church leadership and asked if they could use our facilities as a designated shelter in case of weather-related emergencies.

"Of course," my pastor husband said. Our central location, large gym, and well-stocked kitchen made our campus ideal. But how could we plan for an event that most likely wouldn't happen? We kept certain items in stock for such an emergency. But we knew, beyond that, we would have to trust God to provide.

And he did. Above and beyond what any of us could have imagined. When the blizzard hit, word spread within half an hour to the entire community that the church was open. The fire department started bringing to the gym everyone stalled in a snowdrift, from holiday travelers to local nurses en route for their night shift at a regional hospital. One family walked over the leftovers of their Thanksgiving dinner. Another walked to our small town's convenience store to wipe out the store's supply of doughnuts. Yet another went to buy food for the four dogs that had arrived with their owners. The church's ladies' group had recently finished making lap robes for the local nursing home and for some odd reason, we hadn't been able to connect with the nursing home to get those blankets delivered. But we had them that night to distribute to the travelers. God knew when and where those blankets needed to be.

Our church family knew we could not take credit for what happened. All we did was unlock a few doors. We saw the miracle unfold before our eyes. For one night, perfect strangers from all walks of life and different ethnic groups coexisted, shared blankets, worked together to cook food, and helped each other dig out cars from snowdrifts. One woman, heading home after Thanksgiving with her family in another state, had followed her GPS directions across country roads. When her car skidded into a snowbank, she couldn't tell the EMTs where she was. Suddenly, the swirling snow thinned, and she said, "It looks like I'm at a crossroad of a divided highway and I see flashing lights."

"We see you!" they responded. The team had been scouring the highway that paralleled our small town, looking for stranded travelers and had just arrived at that juncture five miles north of town.

The storm was scary, but watching God at work through a group of people was exhilarating. Even so, we didn't realize the impact the story would have on others. One post on Facebook was shared to other pages sixty times. The church office received letters from out-of-state family members saying in essence, "We were praying that God would provide for our family member, and he answered our prayers through you."

Bad news is the bread and butter of journalism. Tension and catastrophe catch attention. Bad news also plants despair. People crave good news. We love the story of an underdog who defies the obstacles to overcome. That's what the blizzard represented: hope to a despairing world. Hope for others, that if they ever got caught in a life-and-death situation, God would partner with his people to provide rescue—like he did with the little church in the middle of nowhere that sheltered seventy people and four dogs.

In our current world situation, media outlets don't have to look far or fabricate much to report bad news. But as Christ followers, we know that God is bigger than the bad news. Crises and catastrophes are merely invitations for the Lord to demonstrate his love and mighty power to provide through his people. And I've often noticed that when the world is at its worst, the Lord's work is at its best. Nations clash against nations while food pantries across the country quietly feed those caught in financial crisis and spiritual revivals ignite at public universities.

> Crises and catastrophes are merely invitations for the Lord to demonstrate his love and mighty power to provide through his people.

Which bit of news will the world hear?

They won't hear it if we don't talk about it, if we don't start the chain of conversation with, "Did you hear?" And we can't report it if we don't partner with God to make the news. It doesn't take much. Sometimes, it's no more than allowing blizzard winds to press us into a door and praying as we unlock it, "Lord, give me what I need to do what you need done from this point."

You hear best from the front row, because that's where you will see and hear the finer details that don't make it into the newspapers. You'll see God do amazing things with the little that you have. And you'll hear the response of the audience behind you as they witness the goodness of God through the work of his people.

You'll hear them say, "Did you hear . . . ?"

Lord, choose me to be front and center in your next good news story. Use me to convey your message of hope and healing to those who desperately need it. Let them hear how you are in control over whatever happens in our world.

········· LISTENING WITH OPEN EARS ···········

What good news can you pass on through word of mouth or social media? Choose a good news story you know about and pass it on.

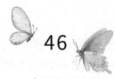

46

Witty and Wise Words

She speaks with wisdom,
and faithful instruction is on her tongue.
PROVERBS 31:26

*E*very mom has a collection of witty sayings her children can recall, though she doesn't necessarily remember saying them.

My mom had several.

"Spinach will make you strong."

"Coffee will stunt your growth."

"Burnt toast will make your hair curl."

I laughed at that last one. My hair was straighter than a sewing needle. Pass it over.

Lest you think my mother thought only of food, she had other sayings that have acted like guiding lights throughout my life.

"Nothing ventured, nothing gained."

"You have not because you ask not."

My daughters say I've passed that last one on to them. *Have I?* They also remember one maxim I intentionally said many times: "It's the process, not the product." It didn't matter if our cake-decorating project ended up in a slithering pile of goo. If we had fun, bonded with each other, and learned from what we did, I wanted them to know the cake was a success, even if we threw most of it away.

I've caught those who've come behind me repeating my words. My older daughter modified that last proverb for her own children, saying, "The fun is in the doing." One church member told me how she encouraged a friend: "I told her my pastor's wife always says, 'God's timing is perfect.'" Another friend, watching a tragic situation unfold before her, wrote how I always talked about looking for God's redemptive power. I guess I've voiced similar thoughts elsewhere because my younger daughter remembers me saying, "God wastes nothing." I'm not original. That came from one of my own mentors.

Our Lord wants us to use words that do more good than harm. He also wants us to use words that have more than a moment's impact. He invites us to speak wise words into the lives of others, words that remain long after we've left.

The prophet Jeremiah wrestled with God's calling on his life to prophesy to the people of Israel. God asked him to do a tough job: speak of God's ways even while watching God's people suffer the punishment for their many sins. In Jeremiah 15, God reiterated his calling: "If you repent, I will restore you that you may serve me; if you utter worthy, not worthless, words, you will be my spokesman. Let this people turn to you, but you must not turn to them" (v. 19). When we take on God's eternal perspective and accept his directive to point others toward faith in Jesus, we become spokespeople for God. Every sentence we say is more than a decision to avoid harmful words. Every word needs to count for God's kingdom. He invites us to utter words with lasting impact: *worthy, not worthless, words.*

That's what I want, to speak worthy words. I think all of us do. We want to leave a lasting, beneficial impression on those who hear us. And if we are people of faith, we want those words to align with God's Word.

Sure, there's nothing wrong with "Spinach makes you strong." But how can we really make our words count? How can we make sure we'll speak words of wisdom to the next generation of children and believers? How can we say worthy, not worthless, words?

Get close to Jesus. Seek his face always. Devour his Word. Fill your mind, heart, and life so much with his ways that they become a part of who you are. If you want to say wise words, then become wise yourself. Proverbs 4:7 says, "The beginning of wisdom is this: Get wisdom." It sounds so simple, so obvious, but it's so true. Later, in the same chapter, the writer says that everything flows from our heart (v. 23), so if our heart is right with God, the words that come from our mouth will be the right words.

He invites us to speak wise words into the lives of others, words that remain long after we've left.

While memorable sayings spill from our mouths at unpredictable moments, we can still have some intentionality in the matter. When I struggled with perfectionism, for example, I concluded that the process was more important than the end result, and I decided that was a message I wanted to impart to my children. It became such a part of me that I actively looked for opportunities to insert that wisdom into whatever we did. We didn't plan to make a mess of a cake, but when we did, it became a teachable moment, allowing me to tuck wisdom into their souls. And saying the words was as much a reminder for me to back off from the pursuit of perfection as it was for them.

What messages do you want to leave the next generation? How can you be sure they are listening? If you have wrapped your life with the ways of God, then the words that spill from your mouth will be words of wisdom, words worth remembering. Stay in close contact with your Lord and pray that he uses your mouth to speak worthy words to the people he's brought into your life.

Lord, fill my mouth with wisdom and my heart with understanding so I may speak of your ways to those who hear me.

········· LISTENING WITH OPEN EARS ···········

At the end of your life, what three sayings would you like others to remember you have said? Write them down. Pray that God will give you chances to speak those truths into the lives of the people closest to you.

47

Love Notes

I have loved you with an everlasting love.
JEREMIAH 31:3

I first heard my mother say "I love you" when she was eighty-seven years old, her mind clouded with dementia, and only in response to my saying the words first.

Mother came from a family who spoke their love through actions. I knew she loved me. She fought for me to stay in public school when school officials threatened to send me to the state blind school. We had little money for gas, but one January afternoon, she drove me all over east Tucson to buy the chess set of my dreams with Christmas money I'd received—even though none of my family or friends played chess. And whenever I was sick with a bad cold, she would buy me pineapple juice. Those were the days before science proved warmed pineapple juice relieves congestion and cough; she just bought it because she knew I liked it and it made me feel better.

I'd heard other families say the words "I love you." I wondered what I was missing and why hearing the words disclosed a deeper craving than the one I had for chocolate. Jack also came from a House of the Unspoken Words, and we determined we would say "I love you" to each other and our children often. The singsong chant became part of the nightly routine: "Mommy loves you, Daddy loves you, but Jesus loves you most of all."

Yet my mother remained silent.

As time passed, I drifted into the habit of saying "I love you" to my husband and children just because that's what we said. Worse yet, I sometimes caught myself saying these words to my family while hoping they'd return the phrase I felt long overdue to hear. Yet, as I listened to others outside my family use the words, I sometimes caught hints of insincerity—people who said the words, but whose actions didn't live up to them. Like the time a church couple told my husband and me how much they loved and appreciated us but, two weeks later, publicly trashed our motives and methods of ministry. When those people said, "I love you," I wanted to scream, "Don't bother!"

I recalibrated my understanding: The words by themselves were not enough.

Perhaps Mother was right. Maybe the actions were the important part of the equation of expressed love. Still, I reasoned, actions didn't tell all. It's easy to slip into the mindset of one husband whose wife asked, "Why don't you tell me you love me?"

"I told you on our wedding day," he said. "If anything changes, I'll let you know."

Or we might model Golde from the musical *Fiddler on the Roof*. She tries to persuade her husband, Tevye, that she loves him by listing all the things she does for him, in the song "Do You Love Me?" Shouldn't we be content with overtures of love spoken through service? Shouldn't actions alone be enough?

No, they aren't. We're human beings. Like Tevye, we have our moments of self-doubt and insecurity, and we need to hear words of love. Actions balance words, and words reinforce the actions. We need both. Hearing it said once isn't enough either. We're forgetful and insecure creatures. We need the reminder that we're loved and cherished for who we are.

My final authority is the opinion and example of God. Did he ever say, "I love you"? Yes, he did in the words of Jeremiah 31:3. But other verses quickly come to mind, showing that God never intended those words to become empty ones.

Actions balance words, and words reinforce the actions. We need both.

> For God so loved the world that he gave his one and only Son, that whoever believes in him shall not perish but have eternal life. (John 3:16)

> But God demonstrates his own love for us in this: While we were still sinners, Christ died for us. (Rom. 5:8)

> See what great love the Father has lavished on us. (1 John 3:1)

> He who did not spare his own Son, but gave him up for us all—how will he not also, along with him, graciously give us all things? (Rom. 8:32)

And unlike my own expressions of love, which can be inconsistent and sometimes stem from questionable motivations, God loves me with persistent, enduring love. He's not ever going away. He will always love me. I have his word on that. I never have to ask "Do you love me?" because he wrote that precious message over and over again in his Word so I wouldn't forget. His actions throughout human history prove he has loved me in the past—and will keep loving me in the future.

Our world has spent thousands of years messing up the meaning of love. We're surrounded by people who don't know how to give or receive it. They've been hurt by others who have loved badly, and their skeptical minds question the motivations behind any words or actions dealing with the topic of love. What a supreme opportunity we have to demonstrate the love of God!

If we are to speak God's concept of love, we'll offer both actions and words with sincerity, pure motives, and faithful consistency. We'll love in the same way he loved us (John 13:34–35). We'll say what we mean, and we'll mean what we say. We'll keep loving even when the other person gets messy, and we'll keep reminding them in their insecure moments that they are loved.

And in our own fallible moments, when our ability to love falls short, we'll remind them, "I do love you, but Jesus loves you most of all."

Because he does.

> *Lord, thank you for telling me and showing me that you love me—and you will never stop loving me. Strengthen me to love others like you do.*

·········· LISTENING WITH OPEN EARS ··········

Read 1 Peter 1:22. Think of someone you will be in close contact with today. Ask God to give you ideas of how to show God's lavish, sacrificial, and consistent love to them.

PART FIVE

SOUND CELEBRATION
What God Hears

48

Musical Expression

Sing to the LORD, praise his name; proclaim his
salvation day after day.
PSALM 96:2

*M*usic is like a thousand-piece puzzle, consisting of myriad sound bites called notes that, when combined with rhythm, pitch, and volume, make one beautiful picture.

No, that's not quite it.

Music is like a box of Legos. Unlike a jigsaw puzzle, where pieces must be arranged in one particular combination to make a complete picture, Legos can be combined into infinite possibilities. Changing one component gives a different look and feel to the finished work. Add the Lego bonus pack of vocal music—with the additional complexity of vowels, consonants, phonemes, words, and four-part harmony— and you exponentially multiply the possibilities.

We still don't have it.

Music is like a candy box. The lining and wrappers provide a structure that holds and presents the treasures of our hearts when mere words seem dull and ordinary. Music is like a glass of wine or piece of fine European chocolate that, when done at its best, leaves you both satisfied and wanting more. You are content to sit and let the present moment pause so you can linger over the loveliness of that treat.

The intricacy and versatility of music amaze me. How humans can combine all these random components into infinite combinations leaves my head spinning faster than a polka. How music affects us is even more astounding. Music gives voice to the breadth of our emotions. Everyone can participate and enjoy the sounds of music. And this powerful structure of sound does far more than entertain. It's a language that reaches across borders, calls us to celebrate the good times in our lives, and informs us that others carry the same thoughts and heartaches that we do.

God did this. He made music for us. He is the author of words and the inventor of sound. He designed our voices to speak and sing, our hands to create instruments that replicate the sounds we hear, and our minds to craft those sounds and words into artistry that . . .

That what?

What are we supposed to do with this enormous gift?

God leaves that up to us. Like all of God's gifts to us, he also gives us a choice of how we use and manage it. Music is a tool that we can use to promote our own agenda or to proclaim God's worldview. We can structure it to manipulate emotions or to help a listener express and process their own emotions. We can use it to please ourselves or to praise our God.

> What are we supposed to do with this enormous gift of music? God leaves that up to us.

And that's the ultimate fulfillment of God's offering. He invites us to use the incredible gift of music to honor him.

God has given us so much in this world for our enjoyment. But he wants to be part of our joy and celebration. He wants to enjoy the music with us. Do we find it hard to tell God and others how wonderful he is through simple words? "Here," the Lord says, "try saying it with music." He hands us another Lego bonus pack, and our souls soar. Like a conductor on a stage, we turn to the masses, lift our hands in praise to God, and say, "Everyone! Sing!" Music stirs us to sing the Lord's praise one more time, as Psalm 96:1 tells us: "Sing to the LORD a new song; sing to the LORD, all the earth."

I'm so glad God gave us music, for music makes it easier to tell God how grateful I am for all he's done and how awed I am of who he is. Like those who linger over wine and chocolate, as a music aficionado, I often find myself focusing on the musical components, worshipping the song rather than its maker. However beautiful and wonderful music is, it's only a tool—a marvelous tool that allows me to give God the most beautiful expressions of praise that I can. And so much more.

Whether or not you participate in music or even enjoy it, it's difficult to imagine a world without it. It's part of the fiber of our lives. The world of music holds so many possibilities for praising our God and so much potential for building his kingdom. And while music has evolved tremendously over the centuries, I suspect we have not even begun to discover the full impact it can have to honor our God.

In these final few chapters, let's explore God's gift of music together.

Thank you, Lord, for creating the gift of music that allows us to proclaim your salvation in so many beautiful, creative ways.

LISTENING WITH OPEN EARS

Listen to one of your favorite pieces of music. Pay attention to the details you normally don't catch. Spend a moment thanking God for creating the complexities that make up that piece of music.

49

Songs of Praise

For you make me glad by your deeds, LORD; I sing
for joy at what your hands have done.
PSALM 92:4

For ten years, I tried to wrap my brain around the concept of grace. I learned mnemonic devices like "God's Riches At Christ's Expense." I sang the hymns. I read the Bible verses. But they were empty words, words without meaning to me.

Then a seminary professor explained God's grace in a way that trickled from my head to my heart, making it personal. I couldn't pay God back for my sin because Jesus had already been to the bank and made a "paid in full" deposit in my account. Grace meant I was free!

I burst into our apartment that evening, my feet barely touching the floor. I two-stepped across the carpet, twirling at midpoint and shouting, "I'm free, I'm free!" Jack's gaping mouth revealed his thoughts. *Class that boring, huh?* My soul ached to sing, "No! I'm free! Praise God, I'm free!"

I've had other times in my life similar to that euphoric moment—when the overwhelming sense of God's power and goodness loosened my emotions in a way that made me break forth in spontaneous praise. The day I heard that a county grant had fully paid our ten-thousand-dollar medical debt in an unprecedentedly short time, and I grabbed the shoulders of my friend Pam in a public parking lot to share the good news. The moment I realized surgery had successfully centered my previously crossed right eye and I could see something other than just my nose. I wanted to burst into several praise choruses all at one time!

Bible accounts assure me I'm not out of line to spill out praise songs in a public parking lot. After God brought the Israelites safely through the Red Sea on dry ground, Moses directed them in a victory song and his sister, Miriam, led the women in a dance party while she played the tambourine (Exod. 15). The prophetess Deborah and her sidekick, Barak, sang together after God delivered the Israelites from their enemies, in a manner public enough that someone recorded the words in Judges 5. And then there's the blind man in Luke 18 who, instead of gawking at all the new things he could see, followed Jesus. His praise was so loud and contagious, others caught the melody of his heart and praised God with him.

We don't have to reserve our praise for Sunday's programmed time slot. Worship can erupt from our hearts any time of the week, whenever we experience God's work in our lives. And God's Word encourages us to mold that excitement in the form of a song. *Sing*, multiple psalms encourage us, *joyfully and loudly*.

> Worship can erupt from our hearts any time of the week, whenever we experience God's work in our lives.

But I don't want my praise to God to be motivated by obligation or because everyone else is doing it; I want to know *why* I'm singing. As I read the context of Bible verses that tell me to sing, I find the psalmists often connecting the command to sing with a reason to do it:

For you make me glad by your deeds, LORD; I sing for joy at what your hands have done. (Ps. 92:4)

Let us sing for joy to the LORD . . . For the LORD is the great God . . . The sea is his, for he made it, and his hands formed the dry land. (Ps. 95:1, 3, 5)

Sing to the LORD a new song, for he has done marvelous things. (Ps. 98:1)

I may not always feel like singing praises to God on Sunday morning as the praise band takes their places on stage. But their organized music leads me into worship and fills the backpack within my heart with songs of praise I can use throughout the rest of the week. Gathering with God's people allows me to hear their excited stories witnessing to God's goodness and greatness. Then, throughout the rest of the week, when I have one of my aha moments or I see God at work in incredible ways, I now have tools I can use to praise my Lord more effectively.

Whether we sing, speak, or think our praise, whether we whisper it in the privacy of our home, join our voices with fellow believers in public worship, or cut loose in a parking lot, God's command is clear on one central point: react to his goodness. Give God the credit he deserves. Do it with excitement, joy, and celebration. Don't hold back. God has given us this incredible gift of song that engages the mind with emotion, and we can use it to powerfully praise him in those moments when we see him with fresh eyes and renewed spirits.

The next time you note how things have come together in your life in a way that can only be attributed to God's handiwork, find a song to sing. Don't hold back. Praise him. Tell of his power and goodness to those who will listen so they can praise God with you. Let the music carry your heart's celebration to the Lord you love. He'll smile and celebrate with you.

*Lord, forgive me for the times I've been shy about
expressing my praise to you. Fill me with enough joy
at what I see you doing that I will want to break out in
spontaneous praise.*

LISTENING WITH OPEN EARS

List five of your favorite praise songs, choruses, or hymns. Keep the list in your Bible or on your smartphone. The next time you find yourself amazed at what God has done or who he is, sing one of the songs on your list.

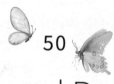

50

Rhythm and Repetition

I will praise the Lord, who counsels me; even at night my heart instructs me.

PSALM 16:7

To my mother's consternation, my stepfather's parents always gave her a small kitchen appliance each Christmas, an appliance that had only one function and in her estimation, a useless one at that. One year it was a hot dog steamer. The following year a bun warmer and the next a hot plate. These appliances, which could be used rarely and only for one thing, took up valuable room in the cupboards and countertops of her small kitchen.

It can be limiting when things have only one purpose.

I'm so glad God made music multifaceted. This beautiful, complex gift can mold into so many melodies. It connects heart, soul, and mind. And it has more functions than merely serving as fodder for a church praise team. For better or for worse, music can entertain, soothe, incite, teach, unite, call to action, and so much more.

Over my life, though, I've appreciated one particular function of music: how it can help us remember facts and concepts we don't want to let slip away. Musical elements, like rhythm and repetition, act as cues that stick the words of a tune in our brains like double-sided tape.

Isn't it wonderful that God gave us melodies that can carry this information, stored in the back of our brains, to the forefront in a fun, enjoyable way?

Early hymn writers latched on to the value of music. In an era when many people were illiterate, hymns taught the basic doctrines of the church. Songs from several centuries ago may seem weighty and wordy to us, but they were a believer's way of remembering basic lessons about the character of God and the need to follow him in faith.

Despite the advent of technology that makes information instantly available, music is often what helps us remember the important. To this day, I remember certain Bible verses because someone put them to song. And I cannot recall the order of the books of the Minor Prophets without humming the midsection of the children's song, "Did You Ever See a Lassie?"

And it gets even better. God uses another element besides music, mind, and memory to help us in our walk with him. He gives us the gift of the Holy Spirit, who works with what's stored in our brains to remind us of what we need to hear at the right moment. When I hesitate to move forward on an uncertain and risky path, Joshua 1:9 comes to mind in the form of a song. When God delivers me from danger, Moses's song in Exodus 15 runs through my head. And in our troubled world that seems anything but peaceful, the Holy Spirit reminds me that only in Christ Jesus will I find peace (John 16:33).

> God uses another element besides music, mind, and memory to help us in our walk with him. He gives us the gift of the Holy Spirit.

Faster than a Bible app on my smartphone, God's Spirit can speak to my soul just what I need at that moment. Many times, when talking to someone who doesn't know Jesus, I've had an appropriate Scripture—

sometimes one I haven't thought of for years—flow out of my mouth. But I've learned that I need to partner with the Holy Spirit in my desire to remember those Bible verses. The more I know about Scripture and the more verses I commit to memory, the more God's Spirit has to work with when he needs to bring that truth to my mind. I'm so glad God orchestrated the teamwork of music and memory that makes recalling the truths and promises of my Lord easier.

If you would like to use music as a memory aid, look for internet resources on Bible verses set to music. If you hear a song at a worship service that speaks to you in a special way, find that song online and play it over and over until you can sing it in your head and heart by yourself. And if you're musically inclined, create your own combinations of Bible verses set to music, as books of the Bible are memorized to the tune of a classic children's song.

Whether you struggle to maintain your relationship with God or with becoming discouraged as you walk with him, God invites you to take advantage of resources he has created to help keep you strong in your faith. You don't have to do it with your own strength. God has provided music, songs, his Word, and his Holy Spirit to help you remember who he is and all that he has done.

Lord, thank you for providing ways to help me remember the important truths about who you are.

·············· LISTENING WITH OPEN EARS ··············

This week, start putting more music in your head. Search for two or three of your favorite songs, or look online for a song your church's praise team sang last week. In quiet moments, sing the words to yourself.

51

Laments

*I will give thanks to the LORD because of his
righteousness; I will sing the praises of the name
of the LORD Most High.*

PSALM 7:17

*M*oments before I left my house to help prepare an Easter breakfast
at my church, a visiting family member ripped open an old heart
wound about a family conflict I had long tried to conceal. Fearing others would see my pain on this happy day, I offered to stir the sausage
gravy when I arrived at church so I could stare at the stove instead
of looking at others. It didn't work; my agony rose like a geyser and
threatened to overflow in the form of tears that would drip onto the
gravy skillet. I turned to what I call my "trouble song," the bit of melody I hum when I feel I have nothing to cling to but Jesus. The minorkey melody is hauntingly beautiful, and the words are from David's
psalm: "You are my hiding place; you will protect me from trouble and
surround me with songs of deliverance" (Ps. 32:7).

"Karen's singing again," one woman commented. *Ah, yes, Karen is
singing but not a happy tune. My friend has betrayed me, and my heart
hurts.* Music muffled the pain and wrapped the message of God's love
and faithfulness with the touch of soft velvet. The melody painted

beauty across the message and infused me with enough courage to lift my eyes from the gravy pan and look furtively toward the group of women with a tremulous smile.

Praise music does not merely stand on the stage of celebration, shouting to the masses about what God has done. It also winds its way to the darkened corners where some worshippers try to hide their tear-stained faces and envelops those who enter the sanctuary with hurting hearts. Music allows us to express what our tongues are not ready to say. The gentle rhythms calm our spirits and the soft melodies act like God's still small voice, reminding us gently that he is in charge and will not allow anything to destroy us.

Music allows us to express what our tongues are not ready to say.

David and other ancient psalm writers penned songs that I wondered about for many years. The songs, known as psalms of lament, speak of David's anguish over the evil in the world. What would make David so despondent? How could he have the gall to ask the Lord God why certain events were happening in his life?

Yet two things are true. First, for David, evil was up close and personal. Dealing with enemies on every side, even within his family and among close friends, was real. How would we react if we had people threatening to kill us, betraying our trust, or seeking to take over the position we thought God had given us? For example, Psalm 7 tells about an enemy named Cush the Benjaminite who evidently had risen up against David. In it, David articulates the thoughts and emotions many of us have experienced but not spoken aloud: "Arise, LORD, in your anger; rise up against the rage of my enemies. Awake, my God; decree justice" (v. 6).

Second, these Psalms of lament are not journal entries. Many of them bear taglines that say, "For the director of music." Psalm 56, which talks about the Philistines' house arrest of David in the city of

Gath, bears that tagline and then holds another part of my trouble song: "When I am afraid, I put my trust in you" (v. 3). The psalm writers intended for people to sing their grief and, within the folds of the songs, recognize the partnership, protection, and power of God to stay with them and save them from evil.

I have my own moments in worship services when I don't feel like clapping my hands, raising my arms above my head, smiling, or shouting "Hallelujah." The best I can do in my hours of lament is raise trembling hands to my waist or clasp them to my chest and, with tears streaming down my face, sing the words anyway.

I think that's okay with God, perhaps more than okay. In an authentic, transparent way, I'm telling my Lord that even though life is tough, nearly unbearable, I will continue to trust him. He is still righteous. He is still so good. He has not forgotten me, and he will be faithful to keep the promises he has made. I believe it enough to sing it.

Are you happy? Are you excited about all that God has done for you? Sing!

Are you beat down? Despairing? Chafing against the unfairness of life and God's seeming silence? Sing anyway. Wrap yourself in the embrace of songs that remind you of who God is. Use the beauty of the melody to salve the sadness of your soul and say what you cannot find the words to say. For when you sing in praise despite your circumstances, you express your faith in powerful, compelling ways, and others will take notice.

Lord, when life becomes overwhelming, you truly are my hiding place. Life doesn't make sense, and my head says it won't get better, but I trust you enough to sing praise to you.

LISTENING WITH OPEN EARS

Do you have a "trouble song"? What one song reminds you of God's faithfulness and goodness? The next time you feel crushed by the difficulties of life, hum the melody to yourself and let your mind savor the words, remembering that God is still in control.

52

World Languages

Sing to God, you kingdoms of the earth;
sing praise to the Lord.
PSALM 68:32

A small Bible training center sat nestled against the Vienna Woods where church leaders from across Eastern Europe and Central Asia came to study and Americans who'd traveled across the Pond served them while they studied. Twice I was privileged to work in the kitchen and mingle with the students.

On the final Sunday of one of my two-week terms, we gathered in the basement that doubled as a classroom and chapel. The worship leader announced we would sing the century-old hymn "It Is Well with My Soul" and encouraged us to each sing in our own language. "We are a group representing fourteen countries," he told our group of over one hundred people. "And among us are seventeen different languages. Let's lift those languages to the Lord."

At first, I found it disconcerting to stand next to someone not singing the same words I was singing. Then I relaxed and listened to the reality of what I was hearing. While we sang in multiple languages, we all sang with the same melody. Music became the common denominator.

Then I listened more closely. We had divided into four-part harmony. Blended together, the four parts became one. Was that how God heard our seventeen languages? To him, was it one balanced sound of praise? I could not understand the words the person beside me sang, but it didn't matter. I was not the recipient, God was. And he could understand. He was the audience of one. We were singing to him, and he finds delight in those who make music in his honor (Ps. 149:3–4). In fact, God accepts our unified praise as a sacrificial gift, for we have openly professed his name—and he takes great pleasure in that (Heb. 13:15).

One hundred people from fourteen countries using seventeen languages and four-part harmony to sing one song, all from memory. The rock-solid message of this song, written by a man who'd suffered tremendous loss nearly 150 years ago, resonated enough with a multinational group of people that we all knew the words. And we all sang from our backdrop of struggles and confidence in Christ's place in our lives.

> God accepts our unified praise as a sacrificial gift and takes great pleasure in it.

We concluded the song, and the worship leader vocalized my growing awareness of the unity we shared. "We are one in Christ," he said. "You are not Americans. You are not Bulgarians or Russians, Romanians or Poles. You are all citizens of the kingdom of heaven."

We were indeed. We all stood on level ground at the foot of the cross. And all of us here on earth share equally in the blessings of our faith and the coming riches of heaven. On that day, we shared more than the solidarity of a melody; our acceptance of the salvation offered through Jesus became the common bond among us. No matter who stood beside me—what country they claimed or what language they spoke—they were citizens of the kingdom of heaven and so was I.

In the first century AD, the Roman Empire ruled the known world. Its citizens were scattered across the countries surrounding the Mediterranean Sea. A person could be considered a Roman citizen in three ways: they were a natural citizen born in Rome, they paid a large amount of money to become one, or, like the apostle Paul, they were the children of a Roman citizen. Paul was a Jew by heritage, a Cilician by residence from Tarsus, yet a Roman by citizenship. This gave him special privileges, like the right not to be punished without the benefit of a trial.

Our residence and language may differ from the person standing next to us, yet if we have accepted the salvation Christ offers, Jesus declares us all citizens of the kingdom of heaven and equal members of God's family (Eph. 2:19). What I experienced that one Sunday with residents from fourteen other countries was only a thumbnail sketch of what it will be like when we all come together in heaven to worship Jesus, the Lamb who was slain for the sins of the world. Through giving his lifeblood, he bought back "persons from every tribe and language and people and nation. [He] made them to be a kingdom and priests to serve our God" (Rev. 5:9–10).

If you ever have the chance to join in worship with people who share your faith in Jesus but speak a different language, please do it! And as you sing the same melody with different words, realize you're fulfilling the psalmist's dream: "May the nations be glad and sing for joy, for you rule the peoples with equity and guide the nations of the earth" (Ps. 67:4). You'll experience in real time that God's gift of music and, greater yet, his gift of salvation were meant for all people, whoever they are, whatever language they speak, and wherever they come from. Through Christ, we are one.

Oh Father God, thank you that your message of love
and salvation is for all people, no matter what language
we speak. Thank you that despite all our differences,
we are one in you, and we share that common
hope and common faith.

················· LISTENING WITH OPEN EARS ·············

Look on the internet for a familiar praise song or hymn sung in a
different language. Listen to the song all the way through without
looking at an English translation. Praise God that he understands all
languages and loves praise from all people groups.

53

Praise Prompts

*I will sing of the LORD's great love forever; with
my mouth I will make your faithfulness known
through all generations.*

PSALM 89:1

I inherited my passion for playing the piano from my great-
grandmother who never played a note in her life.

Stepping into Grandma Belle's house was like backtracking into history by fifty years. Grandma still used a wringer washer, and her dresses came from the old ladies' rack at Montgomery Ward. I never did see her in a pair of pants. A rough-hewn quilt frame bearing her latest project spread across the two twin beds in her guest room, and her yard was filled with sweet-smelling citrus trees. To this day, I remember the year the lemon tree had a bumper crop of over fifteen hundred lemons. She made us count every one.

Grandma told stories of her Scottish father making handmade brooms while singing in Gaelic. She'd also learned some German from her immigrant husband and, in her early eighties, could still sing the Christmas carol "Silent Night" in its original language.

Grandma would come to our house and ask me to play "Stille Nacht" on the piano. She sat beside me on the bench and sang all the

German words. She would then pat my hand and say, "You have nice piano hands. You have long fingers." She held up her stubby ones. "Not like mine." The truth was, she explained, her family could never afford a piano. But she always wanted to play. She and her sisters would sit on the doorstep stoop and tap their fingers on their knees pretending to play the piano.

I could relate to that story. Many times I had lain awake at night, splaying my hands across the quilt Grandma made for me, pretending to play tunes of my own making or practicing passages I had learned in piano lessons. Grandma said I would be a good piano player. And if Grandma said so, I wanted to prove her right. So, because of Grandma's words, I worked hard to be the best pianist I could be.

I cherish the memories of others who have spoken into my life. The second-grade teacher who, upon choosing me to participate in the school's Christmas choir, said, "You have a good singing voice." A sixth-grade substitute teacher who read an assignment I wrote and then told me, "You need to keep writing." *I will—with joy!* Mary, the wife of our preacher, who told me I would make a great pastor's wife. At the time, I didn't react graciously to her opinion, but when my husband began his first ministry, her stray comment gave me confidence that I could do the preacher's wife thing.

The world is a new place for our children, full of beginnings. Their little minds are constantly busy: learning, organizing, and categorizing all that makes up our world. They're finding their place: what they can do, what they find interesting, and what they want to learn about more than anything else. Some kids flit from one activity to another, trying to find what they do well, what is the easiest thing to do, or what is worth putting extra effort into achieving.

Comments we may never remember saying can glow in a child's memory till their passion ignites. The simple love of a song and our willingness to share it might kindle their interest in something they've wondered if they could do.

As Christ followers, we can add a spiritual dimension to the pursuit of their passions and development of their gifts. Paul did that with a young disciple named Timothy, the son of a Jewish woman and a

Greek man. Recognizing that Timothy had inherited the rock-solid faith of his grandma Lois and his mother, Eunice, Paul encouraged him to "fan into flame the gift of God" that Timothy had received when Paul laid hands on him (2 Tim. 1:6).

> Comments we may never remember saying can glow in a child's memory till their passion ignites. It might kindle their interest in something they've wondered if they could do.

That's what we can do with our kids, whether they're ours by blood or ours in the faith. When we see a flicker of interest or spark of talent, we can point it out and remind our young friend that their gift is from God. We can give them ideas of how they can use their gifts for God's glory and offer them chances within the Christian community to use their gifts to serve others and honor God. Simple words like "You're doing so well" or "You could become . . ." might set them on the path God has planned for them, whether it's through music or other ways that best use their abilities.

Who are the children currently within your sphere of influence? What potential do you see within them—art, music, sports, people skills, cooking? Tell them. Remind them it's a gift from God. Give them ideas of what they could do with the gift. And if you get the chance, sit on a bench with them and enjoy those first faltering attempts, continuing to remind them of what they can become.

You may never know what God might do with the sound of your song—even if you sing it in German.

Lord, raise up a new generation of young people who love you, know you, and want to honor you with the abilities

you have given them. Show me how I can encourage them
to become all you have planned for them to be.

·········· LISTENING WITH OPEN EARS ··········

Select two children you know. As you think about who they are, what they're interested in, and what you see them doing well, brainstorm ways you can encourage them. Don't know what to do? Plan to spend more time with them so you can observe their growing interests and abilities.

54

Notes of Encouragement

Therefore encourage one another and build each
other up, just as in fact you are doing.
1 THESSALONIANS 5:11

*G*reat-Grandma Belle gave me the passion to play the piano; Deacon Doug gave me tools to make it happen.

I've long said that God imparted the gift of music performance to some people and the gift of music appreciation to others. Musicians are not complete without an audience. We need those who love to listen to our music and say with obvious enjoyment, "Oh, play it again."

That describes Doug, a deacon in my childhood church. I was only sixteen when my church asked me to play the grand piano for Sunday morning worship services. In those days, it was our practice for the deacons to pass large wooden plates to collect the offering while the pianist played a solo. That was me. And I started to notice, whenever I played a certain old hymn, "Beyond the Sunset," Doug would round the corner by the piano, whistling the melody. I admit, I played that song often just so I could hear him whistle.

Doug's enjoyment of my music apparently went deeper. One evening, when we stopped by the home of Doug and his wife, Sandy, he drew me into the living room. "Play the piano for me, please." I launched into one of my classical pieces. His applause was in the form of a long, deep sigh. "Oh, play some more!" He genuinely enjoyed my music. That fed my faltering confidence like you can only imagine.

One Sunday, the music program was particularly grueling. Doug and Sandy found me rubbing my eyes at the end of the service. "What's wrong?" Sandy asked.

"I have a headache," I said, then admitted the truth. "I always have a headache after playing the piano."

"Do you play by ear?" she asked.

"No, I read music." I explained how I had to lean close to see the music on the rack, which put my entire body at an awkward position. I told about the wooden rack my grandfather had built for my home piano that brought the music up and out so I didn't have to lean over to see it. "It's custom-made for my piano so it won't fit the piano at church."

Doug stroked his chin. "Bring your rack to church next Sunday." I didn't know at the time that Doug was a carpenter by trade and a woodworker by hobby. The following Sunday, he examined my rack, asked me to position myself on the piano bench, whipped out a measuring tape from his pocket, and scribbled some measurements on the back of the church bulletin. Within a month, Doug and Sandy had presented me with a beautifully handcrafted wooden rack, customized to fit that grand piano so I could play for church services with greater ease.

Doug appreciated the gift I had. He encouraged me to keep playing. Then he did what he could to make it possible for me to play.

That's what the body of Christ does for each other.

We give of ourselves and the gifts, skills, and talents that we have. We build each other up by appreciating what others do that we are not gifted to do. And then we do what we can to make their calling from God possible.

The disciple named Barnabas fulfilled that role in the early church. Like the character of Horace Vandegelder in the musical *Hello Dolly*, he believed in helping young things grow. In the early days of the church, Barnabas sold some property and gave the money from the sale to the fledgling church (Acts 4:36–37). He later became aware of the fiery young man named Saul who used to persecute Christians and then accepted God's grace for his own. But Saul was cautious about joining the rest of the Christian community. Barnabas traveled to Tarsus, Saul's hometown, to encourage him to do what God was calling him to do. He made it easier for Saul, whom the Christian world would later know as the apostle Paul, to join ranks with church leadership (Acts 11:25–26). Barnabas did this with his cousin John Mark too. Even after John Mark abandoned the team during Paul's first missionary journey, Barnabas, ever encouraging, wanted to give John Mark a second chance (Acts 15:36–39).

That's what the body of Christ does for each other. We give of ourselves. We build each other up. We do what we can to make their calling from God possible.

Whether it was music, teaching children, working in a community food pantry, starting our first job, or venturing on a short-term mission trip, all of us had a beginning when we hadn't yet honed our skills. We have all made mistakes and experienced faltering confidence. We need people like Doug and Sandy, Barnabas and Horace Vandegelder, who appreciate our efforts, encourage us to keep doing more, and use their own skill set to even out the bumps in our learning curve.

Who is looking for their place in your group of believers? Find ways to appreciate them and make it easier for them to do what they do. If we want to see the church grow larger and stronger, we need to raise up a new generation that is both talented and dedicated to the truth of God's Word. Their rough-hewn efforts need to hear your applause and encouragement to keep going and "do it again."

It doesn't take much. Whistling a song as you pass their corner is a good start.

Thank you, Father, for the people who have paved the way for me to serve and honor you with the gifts you've given me. Show me how I can pass forward the blessing of encouragement to others.

LISTENING WITH OPEN EARS

Select two or three high school or college students you know. How do you see them working or using their abilities to honor God? Find a way this week to encourage them to keep doing what they are doing.

55

Wind Chimes

Just as a body, though one, has many parts,
but all its many parts form one body,
so it is with Christ.
1 CORINTHIANS 12:12

I liked my first set of wind chimes. They added a lovely tinkle of sound outside my window when a bit of cool breeze caressed a warm summer day or provided a touch of beauty to a raw winter's windy moment. The wind caught the clapper of the chimes and beat out its own random rhythm that made me pause and find joy in nature's composed melodies.

Then I sought to buy a second wind chime and discovered that not all wind chimes are created equal. My choices were limited only by how much I was willing to pay. Why were there so many styles? And what about the claim that a particular chime was calibrated to a certain chordal or scale structure? Who paid attention to notes?

Like the tubes of a large pipe organ, wind chimes create a specific pitch and tone based on their length, width, and type of material as the clapper in the middle of the chime activates sound vibrations. Combining certain notes within the musical scale gives a more pleasing sound, especially when they're played randomly by the wind. And to think someone figured this out five thousand years ago, when the Chinese first invented wind chimes to scare birds and ward off evil spirits! The idea and use of wind chimes spread throughout the world and many people, including myself, find them restful and soothing.

Ancient civilizations may have designed the wind chimes for religious purposes, but I find the precision and calibration fascinating. Every design aspect must be in perfect sync for it to work. Each tube needs to be an exact distance from other tubes and attached to the top of the chime structure with strong cords. Each tube responds with its designed tone, does its individual job, but works together with all the other tubes to make a set of notes that function as a unit.

It reminds me of what God wants the church to be.

We are all so different from each other. Each of us holds a unique combination of skills, interests, personality, spiritual gifts, and a customized faith walk. And Jesus prayed for unity? The apostle Paul thought it was possible for us all to work together, to build each other up until we attained the "whole measure of the fullness of Christ" (Eph. 4:13). Really?

Yes. The wind chime is my visual reminder that unity among variety not only works; it's one of God's more brilliant ideas.

No one person can do everything. A wind chime with five identical tubes, all playing the same tone, would become boring. We'd start tuning it out. And God never defined unity as all of us doing and acting the same way. Comparing the church to a physical human body, the apostle Paul says, "If the whole body were an eye, where would the sense of hearing be?" (1 Cor. 12:17). When all the diverse parts work together, the individuality of each person allows the church to accomplish bigger and better things, achievements they could never attain if each person did their own thing. We need each other's differences to bring about the results of our common goals. The more diverse we are, the more we can accomplish.

After an EF5 tornado ripped through Joplin, Missouri, in 2011, two men traveled from western rural Illinois to see how they could help. They returned to their community and gathered a group of people with all kinds of talents. They cast the vision of building a new home for a widow and her three teenaged children. Carpenters, electricians, handymen, and cooks worked for several weeks to erect the house. Those who could not go paid the bills and prayed the prayers. I served as a scribe, recording the events to tell a watching world. College students, with the skill of enthusiasm and the gift of a spring break week, painted the interior. When you look at that home today, it represents the skill sets and faith of hundreds of people, yet the world sees it as one whole structure.

> The wind chime is my visual reminder that unity among variety not only works; it's one of God's more brilliant ideas.

That's what a wind chime is.

That's what the body of Christ—the church—is.

One unit, made of many parts, held together by hard work, a common goal, and many prayers. One whole structure that couldn't come together unless each part was well attached to the head piece, Jesus Christ. Many parts sharing a common goal and a common faith, converging to create beautiful music together that, when done well, the world pauses to acknowledge and admire.

When we offer our unique abilities and perspectives, playing our part in tune with those who work beside us, the church becomes a powerful force. We create endless possibilities of reaching into the heart of the world with the love and grace of Jesus Christ.

The resulting sound is more powerful than the mightiest of pipe organs.

> *Lord, thank you for the package of gifts you've given me and what you've given the people around me. Help us all work well together, each doing our part so we can make great things happen for you.*

··············· **LISTENING WITH OPEN EARS** ···············

What groups do you belong to, in your church, community, work-place, or family? What unique role do you play? How have you seen working with others make even greater things happen?

56

Music Groups

For there is no difference between Jew and Gentile—the same Lord is Lord of all and richly blesses all who call on him.
ROMANS 10:12

When I was a piano student, our local music teachers association sponsored a concert where groups of twelve students took turns playing duets. Each student sat at a grand piano on the community center stage. Six of us played the bass half; the other six played the treble part. While spread apart so we didn't have a chance to know the other pianists, our job was to know our music, listen carefully to each other, and keep our eyes on the conductor.

While I've never participated in a band or orchestra, I've often played duets, accompanied my daughter as she played the French horn, and sung in choirs. I love being a part of a music group. I love that euphoric feeling I get when individuals contribute their voices to create one beautiful, compelling group melody. We are many that make up one.

It takes work for a choir to get to that point. One director told us, "If you can hear yourself but not the person next to you, you're singing too loud. If you can hear them but not yourself, you're too soft." He had us sing one long sustaining note so we could learn to calibrate our volume and pitch to become that one voice. Another director mixed up the four choir parts, not allowing us to stand next to someone singing the same part. We learned to balance our note against the contrasting harmony of the person beside us. It was a bit humbling to let go of our individual voices for the sake of attaining that group sound. But, oh, what a thrill when we finally "got it."

Some of my musical group participations were onetime experiences; others have been long-term commitments where we got to know each other or we knew each other before we combined our musical gifts. In all of these situations, it persistently amazed me how such a mixed group of people from all walks of life, under the guidance of a director, could become a harmonious blend of multiple parts. We combined our various voice ranges to create a voice that spoke as one but represented many.

> It was a bit humbling to let go of
> our individual voices for the sake of
> attaining that group sound. But, oh,
> what a thrill when we finally "got it."

Perhaps that's part of the message the Lord had for Peter that day in Joppa when he saw a vision of a sheet, filled with all kinds of animals, lowered from the sky (see Acts 10:9–16). Peter, a devoted Jew, knew that Mosaic law instructed him not to eat certain animals. But the Jews had carried their exclusiveness so far that they'd disassociated themselves from anyone outside the Jewish nation. Not so for the new church, the Lord made clear to Peter. The Gentiles, who represented all the races of the world, would be included in God's family. Everyone would belong. Everyone would sing together. "There is neither Jew nor

Gentile, neither slave nor free, nor is there male and female, for you are all one in Christ Jesus," Paul would later write in Galatians 3:28.

I think of the people Jesus welcomed into the new kingdom of God. The Samaritan woman, an outcast within her own community because of her multiple marriages. The tax collector Zacchaeus, snubbed by the Jews for his job choice and association with the Romans. Mary Magdalene, a woman with seven demons living within her. Jesus met them, accepted them, and transformed them into people who bore his image well. Those were the faces that lined the dinner table of the newly established church.

God includes everyone in his choir of praise.

As I've sung with everyone from a retired army sergeant to a teenager younger than my daughters, with people from vastly different socioeconomic backgrounds, experiences, and emotional burdens, I've come to dearly love people I might not have otherwise sought out to befriend. Music taught us how to cooperate, and our shared love for Jesus gave us something to talk about after the music faded away.

Choirs are less popular today, and many of us may not have the time or inclination to be involved in a music group. But any kind of shared work—within a church, neighborhood, or extended family—has the potential to create common bonds. Like the work of any choir, getting along takes practice, lots of practice. We hit snags and discord. We have bad days where no one feels like doing the less desirable or monotonous tasks. We have our own ideas of how the group can reach our goal and we question the leader's ability. We squirm beside the person who sits next to us, secretly wishing we could have a seatmate who's more like us. But as time passes, the snags become easier to unravel, talk is more harmonious, and we find ourselves less disagreeable as we see glimpses of the results of our shared work.

How do we reach that goal of harmonious oneness? We seek to know God's message through the pages of the Bible. We connect with each other so we can help each one grow and become strong. We keep our eyes on Jesus, the author and perfector of our faith (Heb. 12:2). And as we keep coming together, mixing our lives with each other, the song the world hears from us will become more distinct and alluring, to the point where those on the sidelines will say, "See how they love one another!" (see John 13:35).

One day we'll reach the other side of God's transformation of his people. We'll discard our final shred of differences and stand before the King of Kings, praising him with one harmonious voice. For now, the music of this earth invites us to practice for that time when we'll stand as one for the most amazing praise performance ever.

The unity will be more incredible than anything we can possibly imagine.

Thank you, Lord, that you look beyond earthly distinctions and count us all as equally loved and valued in your sight. Help me express that acceptance to those who, though they may be different by earthly standards, share the same faith in Jesus.

LISTENING WITH OPEN EARS

How much do you associate with people from different ethnic, generational, racial, or socioeconomic backgrounds? Ask God to help you connect with people you consider different from yourself and show you how the two of you can share a similar melody of life.

57
Off-Key Notes

Shout for joy to the LORD, all the earth.
Worship the LORD with gladness; come before him
with joyful songs.
PSALM 100:1–2

I was ready to worship God, eagerly looking forward to singing his praises. But as I settled myself in a seat near the front of our church auditorium, a group of rowdy upper-elementary-age kids tromped down the aisle and plopped in the seats in front of me. Sensing there wasn't room for her, one of the girls circled the rows and sat next to me. So much for my undisturbed time of worship.

I leaned forward to address the group. "You know if you sit by me, you'll have to pay attention," I said. I was trying to keep it light; after all, I was a teacher in the children's ministry. Couldn't I get away with saying something like that? But their eyes grew wide, their mouths hung open, and they scooted out as quickly as they had scooted in.

All except one girl, who stayed planted beside me. A quiet middle schooler with a troubled home life, Sarah also struggled with a severe learning disability. We'd tried many times to reach out to her family, so I was grateful she had sought me out. Dreams of showing her a godly example of how to engage with God during worship skittered through my brain.

But the dreams left as quickly as they had arrived. And Sarah taught me more that day than I suspect I taught her.

She sat silent until we came to the third song, and then she started to sing. Her croaking, off-key voice trailed two beats behind everyone else, and it had the effect of throwing off my own vocal precision. I ignored the wisdom from former choir directors who'd taught us that if we couldn't hear the person next to us, we were singing too loud. I sang louder.

It didn't work.

By now, you may have guessed that I love music and I have had my fair share of training and musical experiences. I have a reasonably good singing voice and I work hard to sing the best I can. After all, doesn't God want our best? Do you hear a musical motif of pride in here? You should.

Lord, how can I sing my best for you when someone else's voice is throwing me off-key? I prayed.

But what is God's definition of best? The thought hit me as hard as an unexpected clash of cymbals in an orchestra performance. The Holy Spirit wouldn't leave me alone, for another question entered my brain. *What does God think of Sarah's singing efforts?* After all, this praise session was about him, not about me.

God gave us the ability to worship him. He designed the basic structure of music and put within his human creation the capacity to develop, articulate, and mold music into forms that creatively express our emotions and our praise. But people, not God, have devised standards that define what is and isn't good music. It is people, not God, who have determined what they believe constitutes musical perfection.

We say we want to give our best to God. But God has a different set of standards for the "best." He looks at the heart and attitude of the worshipper, not the caliber of the singing voice. He wants whatever we do to come from a heart of joy and adoration.

"Let everything that has breath praise the LORD," says Psalm 150:6.

Everything. Not just a select group who sing prettily or have a knack for playing an instrument. And the psalmist gets more specific: "May the poor and needy praise your name" (Ps. 74:21). That means anyone, any way they can, even those who don't have access to musical training, don't speak eloquently, and can't find the right words.

God wants whatever we do to come from a heart of joy and adoration.

Jesus once used a widow's offering as a real-life object lesson (see Luke 21:1–4). The woman gave two pennies to the offering plate. Giving tithes and offerings was considered as much a part of the worship experience as singing praises. Pennies were next to nothing compared to the treasure boxes of cash wealthy worshippers dumped into the offering bin. Yet Jesus praised the widow's offering because "she out of her poverty put in all she had to live on" (v. 4). She gave her all, even if it wasn't as much as others were putting in.

I looked at Sarah. Her body leaned forward, fully attentive to the worship moment. Her face glowed. She seemed to have no self-consciousness about her voice. She *was* singing her best for God. She was in her safe place, she was participating, and she was filled with joy. And God was pleased. For to him, praise from any of his creatures is more heavenly than the scent of fresh-baked brownies, a garden of orchids, or grilling meat.

God cares more about the purity of our hearts and the gratitude behind our words than he does about the clarity of our singing voice. Psalm after psalm invites me to sing, not because I enjoy singing or because I'm good at it but because God has done great things, I've a story to tell in song, and God's love endures forever.

That should become the motivation behind my song. After hearing Sarah, I now long to reach the point where I'm so enraptured with all that God has done that I forget how I sound, who hears me, or how beautiful the music is. Instead, I want to abandon myself and think only about our great and glorious God.

Do you hesitate to sing because you don't think you sound good enough? Please sing anyway. If you are moved to lift your voice in praise to your God, do it. He is the audience of one and he will revel in your offering of praise and gratitude. He cares most about the motivation behind your praise, and if you sing out of heartfelt gratitude, he is delighted.

Oh Lord, forgive me for the times I have thought more of myself than of you when I join with others to sing your praises. Help me reach the point where I forget about myself and focus entirely on who you are and all you have done.

LISTENING WITH OPEN EARS

Read Hebrews 13:15–16. What kind of sacrifices please God? Why would these actions please God more than the use of our musical talent in praising him?

58

Heart Melodies

But we have this treasure in jars of clay
to show that this all-surpassing power is from
God and not from us.
2 CORINTHIANS 4:7

*G*od had a growing reputation for sending reminders of his presence within the people who sat beside me in public worship services. Sarah was one. My friend Duke was another.

Duke was one of those people we would label as a work-hard, play-hard, die-hard kind of guy. If he had his druthers, his diet would consist of Little Debbies for breakfast and cheeseburgers for supper with several Pepsis throughout the day. Watching him work long hours on his farm in western Illinois, many of us said Duke would be the one who dropped from a heart attack on the back acreage of his pastureland. In Duke's own words, nothing would've made him happier—work one moment, heaven the next.

It was not to be.

Duke started to stumble on steps and stutter out words. Within two years, this active, fun, gracious, and generous man was entrapped in a wheelchair in a care facility bearing the diagnosis of ataxia dysarthria, a kind of dementia that primarily affects speech and motor skills.

Long before Duke faltered, he told me that his favorite hymn was "How Deep the Father's Love for Us." It was the perfect song for him. Duke had chosen to follow Christ in midlife, and the life change was phenomenal. This was a man who understood the deep love of Christ and imitated it in every way he could. And, despite having no formal musical training, Duke sang with a gorgeous, resonant tenor voice.

Duke and his wife sat beside me one of the last times he attended worship services at our small church. I quietly hoped we would sing his favorite song—and we did! But would Duke remember it? I didn't know how much his condition affected his memory, and surely his speech was altered enough that he wouldn't be able to sing even two beats behind the rest of us. But Duke sang every word of all four verses—every note a perfect one.

Hearing Duke sing was a special moment, especially after we'd watched him decline so rapidly. And I believe it was the leading of God's Spirit that we happened to sing his favorite song on a week he'd come to worship service after being absent for multiple weeks in a row. But according to scientific research, it isn't so unusual for someone with dementia to recall songs when they're unable to remember other things. Musical recognition happens in a different part of the brain than other memories. I still find it amazing that the human body compensates in that way. When speech fades, the music lingers.

I suspect God intentionally compartmentalized music into a different section of the brain and then connected brain synapses to the speech center, vocal cords, and mouth motions. Music links our minds, emotions, and memories in unique ways that allow us to express our deepest feelings and desires—and nothing runs deeper than our faith commitment to Jesus. When all else was stripped from Duke's life, God designed Duke to be able to express through song the one thing at the core of his life—his deep love for Jesus and his people.

As life fades, we will all experience a stripping away of strength and sensibility. Yet the Lord has left within each of us the treasure of his Spirit pointing toward the eternal. "When the perishable has been clothed with the imperishable, and the mortal with immortality, then the saying that is written will come true: 'Death has been swallowed up in victory,'" says 1 Corinthians 15:54. Death will not have the final word. The song in Duke's soul was an enduring reminder that there is more to life than what is here on earth. We don't need to despair when our earthly bodies begin to break down because, "though outwardly we are wasting away, yet inwardly we are being renewed day by day" (2 Cor. 4:16).

When speech fades, the music lingers.

Do you know someone who is losing their grip on earthly reality? Discover their favorite songs. If you don't know what music speaks to their soul, sing what is familiar to you. Don't be concerned with how you sound. Reach beyond the earthly to the eternal, and speak into the immortal part of your loved one's soul. Look for the flicker of eyelids, the moving of lips, the murmur of words entwined with melody. All speak of something more—their confident faith that one day all of us who believe in Christ will stand and sing with awe-filled voices to the One who will make us whole again.

Sing on, Duke.

Father, thank you for the enduring sound of music
that, when connected with the message of your grace,
powerfully reminds us of our hope in what is yet to come—
the everlasting praise session before your throne.

LISTENING WITH OPEN EARS

What is your favorite praise song? Sing it to yourself. Sing it often. When your life nears the end and you are only aware of one moment in time, that song may surface to bless and encourage those who know you.

59

New Songs

I will sing a new song to you, my God; on the ten-
stringed lyre I will make music to you.
PSALM 144:9

The day after my grandmother's funeral, I attended a church where a flutist played a cherished chorus, "Be Still and Know That I Am God." The hauntingly beautiful notes of the flute connected with my troubled heart in ways singing the song would not have done. From that day on, I wanted to play the flute, to learn it well enough that I could reproduce the performance. Since a performer holds a flute to the side, I figured I'd be able to lean in close to see my music, which isn't possible with other band instruments. And I knew music theory, so learning the flute would be easy.

Not as easy as I thought, as it turned out.

In my midthirties at the time, I was distracted from this bucket list item by other life activities. It took me fifteen years to purchase a flute. Another ten years to find a teacher. I was getting older and losing breath control. I had no clue how to spell *embouchure*, much less adjust my mouth into the proper position. Finally, after my husband retired and we moved to our current home, I unpacked my flute and found a teacher, a book, and time to learn five separate, halting notes. It wasn't

enough to play the "Be Still" song, but I could figure out other choruses with a repertoire of five notes. And my soul soared. As I played
the chorus "God Is So Good," I thrilled at the beauty of the music and
rejoiced in the goodness of God. The simple words of a familiar song
took on new meaning and drew me closer to my God.

I've long puzzled over the psalmists' direction to "sing a new song"
(see Pss. 33, 96, 98, and 149). Did David and Asaph, the musical directors of the Old Testament, expect us to sing original compositions
every Sunday? What's wrong with singing the hymns I've sung since
childhood?

Nothing.

But the familiar runs the risk of becoming rote. When I enter God's
courts of praise with more on my mind than worship of God, it's all
too easy to go on autopilot, disengaging my heart and mind from my
mouth and settling for the ritual of singing. A new song catches our
attention. As we learn the words and melody, our brains invite us to
think about what we're saying and singing.

> The familiar runs the risk of becoming
> rote. A new song catches our attention.

But it doesn't have to be original to be new. Singing a new song can
simply mean finding new and creative ways to express your praise to
God. It might be as simple as listening to or playing the melody on
a different instrument, as I did with the flute. It could be writing an
extra verse to a familiar song that allows you to express the theme in
your own words. You could take an archaic hymn and, in the privacy
of your journal, update the ancient wording to use today's modern
phrases. Ask for a list of the songs planned for the next worship session, look up the lyrics online, and think about the words before you
join your community of believers.

Psalm 33:3 says, "Sing to him a new song; play skillfully, and shout
for joy." God never intended his people to package their praise into a

short list of songs and a limited number of music styles. He designed us to be creative people, with emotions that allow us to respond to what we hear, learn, and experience. God invites us to put effort into our praise by taking the time and initiative to create or recreate, to practice so we can play with skill, to put our heart into it so we praise with joy, and to sing and play loudly—even to shout—so others hear and notice.

If you are not into music, you can find other creative ways to praise God: poetry, art, or photography, to name a few. Nature walks can lead to all kinds of praise moments. You can incorporate praise into your prayer time and include prayer in your everyday moments. Go through a praise list while you are doing "mindless" tasks. Sing or shout praise sentences while you vacuum or when you are driving by yourself.

Whatever you do, remake praise so it's new and fresh to you. Don't allow the old to become stale. Your faith and understanding of God are always growing and evolving. You have new stories to include in your faith testimony. Your list of praise points is growing longer. As these things happen in your life, your praise to God should reflect your reactions to what you see. Searching out new ways to sing the old familiar songs will give you tools to express your new awareness of God's work in your life.

And as you find new ways to praise and proclaim your faith in God, others will hear. The changes will catch their attention, just like a flutist caught the attention of a grieving visitor one Sunday morning two decades ago.

Lord, you are worthy of praise. It's worth my time and effort to step out of my comfort zone and praise you in fresh ways. Fill me with creativity so my praise can become filled with joy and gratitude for you.

LISTENING WITH OPEN EARS

What is your favorite praise song, hymn, or Bible verse? Ponder it this week. What is one new way you can express that song or verse so it becomes "a new song"?

60

Trumpets

*Listen, I tell you a mystery: We will not all sleep,
but we will all be changed—in a flash, in the
twinkling of an eye, at the last trumpet. For
the trumpet will sound, the dead will be raised
imperishable, and we will be changed.*

1 CORINTHIANS 15:51–52

The sound of one certain song moves me like none other. I reach for my headphones, lie face down on the floor, and jack up the sound as loud as safely possible. Pure musical ecstasy!

The song? "The Trumpet Shall Sound" from Handel's *Messiah*.

In my imagination, I wonder if the trumpet of the Lord as mentioned in 1 Corinthians 15 and elsewhere in the Bible will sound like the trumpet solo from this aria. *Surely it couldn't be* more *glorious*, I think to myself. I imagine it paired with a particularly stunning sunset, light beams ripping apart golden clouds to form a perfect circle of intense blue. And I picture my Lord standing in the center, his hand extended, saying, "Come on home!" How awesome is that?

Cue the music, maestro.

The incredible music and pageantry we'll experience when we're welcomed home to heaven will be tons more magnificent than any painting or performance you or I have ever experienced. I don't know a fraction of the logistics behind Jesus's return—like how the entire world will see and hear his entry all at the same moment. But I do know the choreography will be so spectacular that we'll all fall to our knees in worship and acknowledge who Jesus is—the King of Kings and Lord of Lords.

> The incredible music and pageantry we'll experience when we're welcomed home to heaven will be tons more magnificent than any painting or performance you or I have ever experienced.

The music geek inside me wonders: Will the trumpet be a *recitative*? Will it be a celebration sound like a happy wedding march signaling the coming of the bride? Or will it be one long blast that sounds like the warning of an amber alert or air raid siren? Will it fill those who have rejected the one true God with utter dread as they realize how wrong they've been about Jesus's identity and call to salvation?

The story of Joshua's army marching around Jericho gives a clue to how the world might react to that trumpet sound. When the Israelites were ready to enter the promised land, the city of Jericho was shut up tight because the residents were so afraid of the Israelites and their God. For six days, Joshua's army marched once around the outer perimeter of the city walls, trumpets announcing their progress. On the seventh day, the army marched around seven times. Then the trumpets gave one ominous blast, and the Israelite army let out a loud shout. At that moment, the city walls collapsed (see Josh. 6:1–27).

I can imagine that most of the city dwellers were terror struck. Those walls represented the last of their defenses. Life was over for them, and they knew it. But not for all of them. For the family of Rahab, a woman who'd previously hidden two Israelite spies, that trumpet blast represented liberation, as they were spared by the army (vv. 17, 23, 25). Defeat for some; deliverance for others.

The final sounds on earth, according to 1 Thessalonians 4:16, will be the voice of the archangel and the trumpet of God. The dead who claimed Christ as Lord will come back to life, and those of us alive at the time of Christ's return will gather with them in the clouds to meet the Lord in the air (1 Thess. 4:17). That means deaf and hearing, people from the past and people in the present, believers of all nations as well as unbelievers—all will hear, and all will react. No one will be able to ignore it. No matter what the trumpet sounds like, the walls of earth will collapse, and life on this earth will be over. All people, past and present, will fall to their knees before the Lord Jesus, realizing without a doubt who he is. But for those of us who've put our faith in Christ, we'll pump our fists in the air and shout, "Yes!" Our deliverance has come.

Are you ready?

If you're a believer, you *are* ready, for you have accepted the salvation Jesus offered when he died on the cross to pay for your debt of sin. For you, perhaps the better question is, Are you waiting? Are you eagerly anticipating his return? Are you looking toward the clouds, expecting Jesus to appear at any moment? Do you hear Jesus's voice in the sound of his people's praises and wonder if the notes of the instruments will turn into that one long trumpet blast?

Are you willing to let go of that craft project, the high school graduation of your children, or your lifelong desire to see the north rim of the Grand Canyon if it means seeing Jesus's return? May we all learn to hold earthly life loosely. For God's final act in restoring creation to what he intended from the beginning of time will be more glorious than anything this world has to offer. And when Jesus comes back to bring his beloved home to the new heaven and new earth, all justice will be served, all wrong will be made right, and all pain will be no more. It will be Better Than Ever, better than the best we've ever known. Better than absolutely anything.

Come, Lord Jesus!

*High and holy Jesus, I'm waiting and longing to hear the
last sound that will ever be heard on earth, announcing
your return. Come quickly to us!*

·············· LISTENING WITH OPEN EARS ··············

What do you imagine you will see and hear when Jesus comes back?
Spend a moment dreaming about what it will be like in that moment
when you see Jesus.

My Prayer for You

*O*h Father God, thank you for the gift of sound and the ability to hear the sounds you have made for our worship, enjoyment, and use.

Help those with hearing difficulties to hear your voice through what they can hear. Help them find praise and gratitude for all you have done in their lives.

Help us all to hear your voice through your Word, the Bible, to pay attention to what you say, and to follow you wherever you call us to go.

Help us manage well what we hear each day. Help us choose wisely what we allow ourselves to hear and what we compel others to hear. Guide us in our use of words and language so we will speak words that honor rather than discredit you, and words that strengthen rather than weaken the one who hears us.

Thank you for giving us the gifts of speech and sound so we can praise you and proclaim who you are to a listening world. Help us all to discover new ways to praise you, for you are worthy of every note of praise.

Finally, Lord, strengthen us and grow in us an ever-increasing desire to hear your final note that calls us home to you. Come, Lord Jesus. Come quickly.

Amen.

Acknowledgments

Do you hear what I hear?

Throughout my life and through the process of creating this book, voices have spoken into my life that added richness and beauty to who I am, encouraged me to be better than I thought I could be, and shared their own ballads that have led me to praise the Lord God Almighty. I am forever grateful God chose to connect my life path with theirs.

I hear the sound of my own voice on the Voice Memos app on my smartphone. Thank you to the inventive person who collapsed the idea of a dictation machine into one small button on my phone. This handy-dandy feature gave me the ability to hang over the side of my bed at midnight to record thoughts I'm sure I would have lost if I waited till morning. And I didn't have to find my glasses, paper, or pen, turn on a light, and wake my beloved while I did a brain dump.

I hear the crunch of dark chocolate–covered almonds. Thank you to those who kept my stash well supplied while I wrote this book. I might have enough left over for the writing of the next book. Maybe.

I hear Jack's lack of comments about my odd behaviors—hanging over the side of the bed, bolting out of the room without explanation, staring off into space, furiously scribbling words on a notepad during sermons that have nothing to do with the sermon, talking incessantly about my latest and greatest crazy idea—and enduring the sound of silence so I could write for hours on end. Thank you, honey. You are indeed a tolerant man.

I hear the vulnerability in the voices of Jack, my friend Kelly, and the cashier at my local dollar store as they share their honest stories of what it is like to not hear well. Thank you all for explaining so the rest of us can better understand your frustration and appreciate your courage.

I hear the sounds of our world, both natural and man-made. Thank you to those who, realizing I cannot always see what I hear, describe the source of the sound. Thank you for patiently answering my many questions, because you also know me well enough to suspect I probably have the ulterior motive of writing about it later.

I hear the encouraging words of my church family, physical family, friends, prayer team members, and agent, Linda Glaz. You all know the rough spots I encountered on this journey, and your words and interest kept me pushing forward more than you know.

I hear the feedback of the wonderful staff at Kregel Publications, who finely tuned the manuscript through the editing process and amplified the message through their marketing efforts. No writer stands alone; it always takes a team. And a great team makes a good book look great. I'm so grateful to all of you.

I hear the praises of God's people. So many have filled my life with songs of God's presence and power. May I give a long overdue thanks to those who have mentored me in music over the span of my life: Mrs. Berk, Mr. Ashcraft and Mr. Moore, Gene, Dorothy, Judy, Elliot, Jolece, Mary Beth, and Donna. These beautiful lovers of music put skill to my song and empowered me to praise God with the tones and rhythms he created.

I hear the voice of God in the sounds of creation and in the words he spoke as recorded by the scribes of the Bible. Thank you, Lord God Almighty, for opening my ears to hear more of what you hear, and to listen to those who struggle with the hearing.

Read more of my discoveries at www.karenwingate.com. And I'd love to hear the sounds you hear: the sounds of creation, the songs of your favorite ways to praise God, and the stories of God's continued work in your life and your corner of the world. Write me at karen@karen wingate.com.

About the Author

Karen Wingate, author of *With Fresh Eyes*, is also a popular speaker, devotional writer, and Bible study leader. For most of her life, Karen was legally blind, until a surgery in 2016 gave her Better Than Ever vision. She and her husband live in Tucson, Arizona. Visit Karen at karenwingate.com.

What do we miss when we close our eyes to the wonder of everyday moments?

With Fresh Eyes invites readers to not only celebrate the gift of sight but also reawaken the wonder of what they observe in creation—great and small—and how God is working in everyday moments. In each of her sixty devotions, Karen Wingate draws a connection between physical sight and spiritual understanding that will leave readers with renewed joy and delight in what is good and beautiful.

KREGEL PUBLICATIONS